MOUNTON HOUSE

The Birth and Rebirth of an Edwardian Country Home

Helena Gerrish

MOUNTON HOUSE

The Birth and Rebirth of an Edwardian Country Home

LUND HUMPHRIES

To my brother Neville, with special thanks and love.

CONTENTS

1.	THE SEARCH FOR A SETTING	10
2.	THE MOUNTON WATER GARDEN	26
3.	MOUNTON HOUSE	40
4.	THE GARDENS OF MOUNTON HOUSE	66
5.	FROM HIGH SUMMER TO WARTIME	88
6.	DECLINE AND FALL	94
7.	THE RECREATION OF A HOUSE	110
8.	THE RESURRECTION OF A GARDEN	160
	APPENDIX Specialist suppliers, craftsmen and designers	200
	BIBLIOGRAPHY	201
	ACKNOWLEDGEMENTS	202
	IMAGE CREDITS	202
	INDEX	203

Preceding images:
(pp 2–3) The solitary seat in the pergola, luxuriantly clothed with roses
(p.4) Watercolour of the pergola, by an unknown artist
(overleaf) The restored front facade and entrance courtyard in spring

1. THE SEARCH FOR A SETTING

The creation of Mounton House and its gardens was the most ambitious project of Henry Avray Tipping (1855–1933), the architectural editor of *Country Life* for almost 30 years and the greatest contributor to the magazine's unique style. Mounton was a new country house in the English tradition and also much more: a show house and garden designed without limitations of expense to be the perfect expression of his immense knowledge of history, architecture and horticulture. All was designed to impress and entertain distinguished guests from the worlds of high society, academia and politics, and after two years of intense labour everything was ready by the summer of 1914. Within weeks the First World War started and the world of English country-house living changed irrevocably; so whether one considers it the result of hubris or completely undeserved misfortune, the fact is that Tipping never saw his hopes for the house come to fruition. In the war years few guests came to see his remarkable creation, the house staff and gardeners he needed were no longer available, and eventually he gave up the estate, settling for a much simpler lifestyle. In time, too, the house was neglected and the magnificent gardens became overgrown. Mounton could so easily have been demolished, just one more of the nearly two thousand lost country houses of 20th-century Britain; and yet, against all expectations, the story of Mounton House is not another tragedy. A hundred years after Tipping completed it, a loving work of restoration of house and gardens was launched, making this a story of redemption.

Tipping (fig.2) was born at the Chateau de Ville d'Avray (fig.3) on the outskirts of Paris shortly before his parents moved to Brasted Place in Kent (figs 4 and 5). His father, William Tipping (1816–1897; fig.6), was the son of a prominent Liverpool corn merchant, a Quaker, and became an archaeologist and antiquary, MP for Stockport, director of several railway companies and a successful promoter and developer of the Westerham and Brasted area for 40 years. His mother, Maria Walker (1822–1911; fig.7) was also from Quaker stock, the daughter of wealthy but socially conscious flax spinners in Leeds. Henry Avray, known to family and friends as Harry, was the youngest of four sons and, after growing up surrounded by the antique furniture and varied collections of Brasted Place and a somewhat eccentric private education, went up to Christ Church, Oxford (fig.8) in 1874. Lady Celia Congreve, whose stepfather had been rector of Brasted, described him at that time as 'slightly bitten by the fashionable craze for aestheticism; he wore his hair long and large flowers, such as hyacinths, in his buttonhole'. He was an actor with the Oxford University Dramatic Society and a debater at the Union, but clearly

1 Picturesque Tintern Abbey above the River Wye, six miles north of Mounton

did not neglect his studies: he took a first in modern history in 1878, at the same graduation ceremony as Oscar Wilde, and was expected to pursue an academic or political career. However, after a short period as a university lecturer, in 1882 he joined the team working under Leslie Stephen on the *Dictionary of National Biography* as a specialist in genealogy; the first volume appeared in 1885 and Tipping wrote contributions related to the Baldocks and Beauforts, the beginning of his intimate knowledge of the British peerage and landed gentry and their historic homes. He continued to live at Brasted but had his own five-bedroom house, The Quarry, built on the estate, and it was here that he designed his first garden. It included the repurposing of an area of quarried ground as a rock garden with stone paths and bridges – a contrast to the highly formal gardens at the main house, which he later wrote of in withering tones: 'There were numbers of many-shaped beds cut out of the lawn, showing bare earth for seven months of the year, and only gay in three. Even then they were not interesting. You walked rapidly round, and said it was well done.'

None of the four sons of the Tipping family married, and in the 1870s Henry lost two of his brothers. Edward Alexander (1852–1871), who was closest to him in age, died of scarlet fever in his final year at Westminster School. The eldest, John Walker (1845–1876), read Law at Trinity

2 Henry Avray Tipping, 1914
3 Tipping's birthplace, the Chateau de Ville d'Avray near Paris

4 Brasted Place in Kent, Tipping's childhood home, designed by Robert Adam, 1748
5 The Tipping family book plate from Brasted Place, Kent
6 Tipping's father, William Tipping, MP for Stockport
7 Tipping's mother, Maria Tipping, née Walker, aged 82, in the loggia at Mathern Palace, Monmouthshire

College, Cambridge, and was admitted to the Middle Temple in 1868; soon afterwards he settled in Saxony and is recorded as dying near Dresden in 'a shooting incident' – which may be a euphemism for suicide. The second son, William Fearon (1847–1911), had a military career, commanding the 3rd Battalion, Royal Welsh Fusiliers from 1886 to 1894, with the rank of colonel from 1893. Tipping's father died in January 1897 so William inherited Brasted Place and its estate and easily assumed the role of squire: he carried out more improvements in the village and became a justice of the peace and high sheriff of Kent. Although Kent was convenient for his work on the *Dictionary of National Biography* in London it appears that Henry found Brasted and the near presence of his parents oppressive. In 1890 he moved to Harbrook Cottage (fig.9) at Ramsbury in Wiltshire, on the estate of Sir Francis Burdett, and in 1894, just before he turned 40, bought his first property in Monmouthshire, the area with which he would be associated for the rest of his life.

The great families of England had always had their historic country estates with magnificent houses which were often barely used – visited perhaps in the summer when the London season was over, or in the autumn and winter for fox hunting or pheasant shooting. Tipping was ahead of his time in choosing to have a weekend escape from London, and in the course of his career as a writer he was to make country living a common aspiration of the wealthy upper middle class. Where they chose to live was often dictated by the routes of railways, so Londoners had their country retreats in the Chilterns, Sussex or the Cotswolds (favoured by Birmingham magnates as well), while northerners might opt for the Peak District, the Yorkshire Dales or the Lake District. Obviously there were other areas which have since

8 The Great Quadrangle at Christ Church, Oxford
9 The cottage at Harbrook on the Ramsbury Estate in Wiltshire, pencil sketch by G.H. Kitchin, 1892

been recognised as national parks or areas of outstanding natural beauty, but they were too remote to be easily reached by train from the city on a Friday evening. Tipping was unusual in opting for South Wales, although it was a logical choice. Alongside the Lake District, the Wye Valley had been recognised as an outstanding example of the picturesque since William Gilpin's *Observations on the River Wye and several parts of South Wales, etc. relative chiefly to Picturesque Beauty; made in the summer of the year 1770*. This was published in London in 1782 and was illustrated with plates based on Gilpin's sketches, using the newly invented aquatint process. Gilpin's touring guides particularly encouraged people to appreciate the rustic beauties of Britain at a time when the Grand Tour on the continent was no longer possible because of the Napoleonic Wars (1803–15). Subsequently small-scale industry, such as paper milling, developed in the Wye Valley but by the end of the 19th century the area had again become predominantly rural, offering both mountains and the beauties of the Severn Estuary, the Wye and the Usk, with the added picturesque benefits of ruined abbeys and castles (figs 1 and 10). Tipping realised that the opening of the Great Western Railway's Severn Tunnel in 1886 meant that the area had become easily accessible from London by train. Up to then passengers between Wales and London had had to take the 'Great Way Round' via Gloucester, but the direct line greatly shortened the journey. This was to prove crucial for his work as architectural editor of *Country Life*.

Up to the mid-1890s Tipping continued work with the *Dictionary of National Biography* but private means also allowed him to travel abroad, spend country weekends with friends and collect antique furniture. By 1894 he had enough money to make a first purchase in Monmouthshire: Mathern Palace (fig.11). The site was not especially beautiful, set just above the levels bordering the Severn Estuary, but it was equidistant between Chepstow and the main-line station at Severn Tunnel Junction; and it had all the

10 *The Junction of the Severn and the Wye*, etching and mezzotint by J.M.W. Turner, 1811

historical associations which appealed to Tipping, having been a residence of the Bishops of Llandaff from 1408 to 1705. The Ecclesiastical Commissioners sold the much-deteriorated property in 1889 to George Carwardine Francis, a local solicitor, and he in turn sold it on to Tipping, perhaps thinking that he had found a gullible customer with no knowledge of the area. Certainly the name and historical pedigree could not disguise the fact that what Tipping bought was little more than a ruin, as he described in an article for *The Garden* in January 1900:

> What remained of the old palace, after the lead had been stripped from the greater part of its roofs, and its interior woodwork and fittings had been destroyed or removed, was turned into a farmhouse. The gatehouse, banqueting hall, and other now useless buildings provided material for barn and cowshed. The chapel was converted into a dairy, the kitchen into a stable.

It was a daunting project to make anything habitable or beautiful out of it, yet by the time of writing this article, after six years of work, Tipping had effected a most remarkable transformation and he lived there for nearly 20 years.

He set himself the highest standards, following the advice of the Society for the Protection of Ancient Buildings, founded in 1877, and aiming to create 'a place of modern residence with as little serious interference as possible with its picturesque aspect and archaeological interest'. That it should be comfortable was essential after his mother came to live with him from 1897 until her death in 1911. Instead of remaining at Brasted Place, her home for more than 40 years, with William, her second son, she chose to spend her old age with Harry, her youngest, and there were certainly advantages for him. Steady financial help from her, in addition to the money he had inherited from his father, meant that the restoration work at Mathern could be both quickly and expertly carried out; and her constant presence at the house meant that a permanent household and gardening staff could be maintained when he was up in London or travelling. The stability provided by his mother also encouraged him to be more social: he visited other grand houses and their owners in the area and had his own weekend and summer house parties for friends from further afield (fig.12).

11 Mathern Palace, Tipping's first Monmouthshire home which he bought in 1894
12 (opposite) Tipping in his loggia at Mathern Palace in 1910
13 (overleaf) The water gardens at Mathern Palace

In a 1910 article for *Country Life* Tipping described the house as an ideal country retreat – 'a quiet home where the simple life may be led' – but it was again worthy of the name Mathern Palace. At the same time he created a garden where before there had been nothing but 'the sordid untidiness of a hopelessly ill-contrived and unrepaired farmstead'. He designed the garden to complement the house, for example with a grass plat to fit into the ruins of the banqueting hall on the east, 'with a bed of dwarf evergreens, heaths and sedums (relieved by gladioli in the summer) which gives some variety of form and colour in the winter at a point commanded by many windows'. There were rock gardens and pathways, terraces bounded by dry limestone walls and spaces defined by yew hedges, and he converted the medieval fish ponds to become a canal with a rustic bridge and grass walk (fig.13). In his 1900 article for *The Garden* Tipping shows his appreciation of the need to match plants to conditions, something that was to be crucial in the varied terrain of Mounton.

Mathern demonstrated Tipping's gift for planning a complex project and also his ability to manage a team – architect, builders, landscapers, gardeners and domestic staff – so that

14 William Robinson, owner of *The Garden* magazine
15 Gertrude Jekyll at Edward Hudson's home, Deanery Garden at Sonning
16 Edward Hudson, founding publisher of *Country Life* magazine

it was carried to completion. At the same time he became part of a very different team in London. In the late 1890s Tipping began writing articles for William Robinson's *The Garden: An Illustrated Weekly Journal of Horticulture in All Its Branches*, which was published from 1872 to 1927, and it is clear that he had long been influenced by Robinson's rejection of Victorian formality in favour of 'the wild garden' (the title of his 1870 book), a parallel to the return to the simple, natural and vernacular which the British Arts and Crafts movement brought to architecture and design. It seems likely that Robinson (1838–1935; fig.14) and his horticulturist colleague Gertrude Jekyll (1843–1932; fig.15) introduced Tipping to Edward Hudson (1854–1936; fig.16), the proprietor of *Country Life*, the magazine that was launched in 1897 after Hudson and George Newnes had bought up *Racing Illustrated* and renamed it (fig.17). Articles on racing and golf were not altogether banished but the focus turned to country-house architecture and gardens, practical gardening, antiques, fine art and books, all with the aim of educating the middle class and taking them mentally, and sometimes in reality, out of their city lives.

The magazine, with its high-quality printing and use of full-page photographs, was an immediate success and Hudson, who was a natural leader in spite of his lack of education, became a very wealthy man. He had a beautiful home at 15 Queen Anne's Gate in London (fig.22) and in 1899 he commissioned his friend Edwin Lutyens (1869–1944) to build a country house, Deanery Garden at Sonning. New offices for the magazine in Covent Garden followed in 1904, and Lutyens later restored Lindisfarne Castle for him. Hudson recognised a kindred spirit in Tipping: they were almost exactly the same age, bachelors (although Hudson married when he was 74), shy but with a gift for close friendships, and with very similar interests. Each of them had protégés who were 15 years younger and treated like sons: the architect Lutyens (fig.19) in the case of Hudson, the architect and artist George Herbert Kitchin (1870–1951; fig.20) for Tipping. Each of them probably also had a sense that they were on the fringes of British society, never entirely accepted because their money came from 'trade'. The furniture historian Ralph Edwards, whose career had been greatly helped by Hudson, cruelly wrote of him as 'the very picture of a prosperous British bourgeois, a typical minor Establishment figure'. The same description could equally have been applied to Tipping. And yet these two, together with a group of talented men and women who were friends as much as colleagues, used the pages of *Country Life* to shape the thoughts and habits of the very society that rejected them.

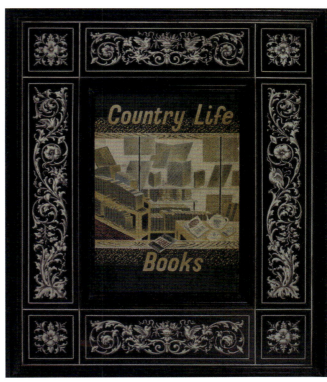

17 First issue of *Country Life*, 8 January 1897
18 Tipping's frame with image of his *Country Life* Books

19

20

21

19 Edwin Lutyens, Hudson's architect and friend
20 George Herbert Kitchin, Tipping's lifelong friend
21 Compton End near Winchester, the home of G.H. Kitchin
22 (opposite) 15 Queen Anne's Gate, Hudson's London home where Tipping, Lutyens and Jekyll met on Mondays
23 (overleaf) Door in coped wall at pergola end of the flagged terrace

2. THE MOUNTON WATER GARDEN

As the century turned and the Victorian became the more relaxed Edwardian age, Tipping's life flourished. He had identified the Chepstow area as the ideal compromise between romantic countryside and easy access to London. He had converted the ruins of Mathern Palace into a comfortable home for his mother and himself and had been able to create an extensive and varied garden. Most importantly, he had discovered a new sense of purpose. From 1903 he began to write for *Country Life*, becoming the architectural editor in 1907 and making a major contribution to Edward Hudson's transformation of a sporting journal into the lifestyle magazine we know even today. He was highly appreciated, Ralph Edwards claiming that Hudson regarded Tipping 'as a veritable oracle', so that Hudson would be 'transformed from a dictator to an obedient slave' in his presence. Bernard Darwin, who commented on golf for the magazine in the same years, wrote that 'Tipping had been, I believe, for some little time a don at Oxford, and something of this seat of learning hung about him in voice and manner. He had an essentially scholarly quality which permeated all that he wrote.' As a good teacher Tipping realised that it would take time to educate his readers. Architecture had originally been an insignificant part of the contents, so he aimed (as he wrote in a reflection in the thousandth issue) to 'begin homeopathically and only increase the dose as the tonic gave strength to the reader's system'. He added that this method 'has succeeded in being educative without being pedantic, informing yet attractive ... Each [country house] has been so treated as to show some merit, teach some lesson, and exercise some influence on the taste of today.' This gentle training of readers' minds was helped by the fact that the magazine came out weekly, and by the reinforcement provided by the series of country-house and garden books that later derived from his weekly articles.

We are fortunate to know something of his pattern of life at this time from his pocket diary for 1908 (fig.25): a rare survival, because he ordered that all his papers should be destroyed after his death. At Mathern he could write up articles on houses which had already been visited and researched but regularly he would go up to London, taking his horse and carriage to the station and then the train in time to have lunch at the Conservative Club in St James's, where he would stay unless he was staying with Edward Hudson. He would spend the day at the British Museum or the London Library, researching the historical, social and architectural development of chosen properties, and he would get permission from owners to visit new houses – where they were rarely resident. There were editorial meetings at the Tavistock Street office (fig.26), gathering

24 The artificial stream and paved path in the water gardens

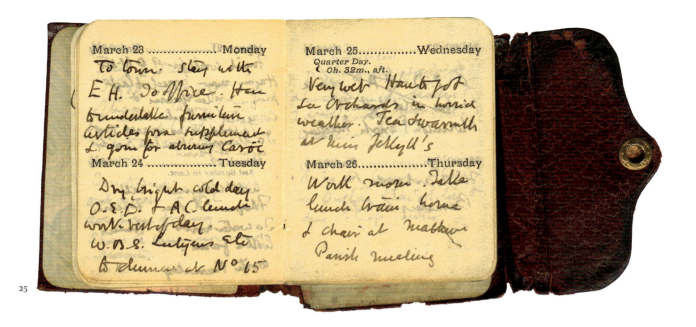

25

26

other experts like garden designer Gertrude Jekyll, furniture specialists Margaret Jourdain, Percy Maquoid and Ralph Edwards, Lawrence Weaver, who covered smaller country houses, and those responsible for property advertising and sports. Many of the same characters would be found dining at Hudson's house in Queen Anne's Gate, or entertaining each other at weekends, because they were both colleagues and friends, aware that they were somewhat on the fringes of respectable society.

The magazine also had articles on the houses of many of these collaborators and their friends – for example Tipping wrote about Ramsbury Manor, on whose estate he had lived, in 1907 and twice more, and he had no awkwardness about presenting his own homes for admiration.

Tipping was more independent than most of the editorial group because his London days were balanced by time in Monmouthshire and visits to notable houses. He was phenomenally hard-working, generally traveling by train but sometimes meeting Hudson's Rolls-Royce and the chauffeur, Perkins, which allowed him to take in a larger number of houses. The 1908 diary reveals 17 houses and towns seen in the course of a five-day tour of the East Midlands in May, and the Rolls only let them down near the very end when it got stuck in the mud on the way to Lyveden. There were similar tours in each of the summer months. Tipping would make notes for the highly skilled photographers Hudson had recruited, Charles Latham, Frederick Evans and, a little later, A.E. Henson; they were instructed to insist on the removal of Victorian furniture which spoilt the view of the house's structure. Fifty-one Tipping articles and their accompanying photographs were published in *Country Life* in 1908, and the value of his work was recognised the following year when he was elected as a fellow of the Society of Antiquaries of London (FSA).

The stimulus of seeing so many grand houses and of meeting regularly with his brilliant colleagues seems to have

25 Tipping's 1908 diary, noting staying with Hudson, dinner with Lutyens and 'tea and warmth' at Miss Jekyll's
26 *Country Life* offices in Tavistock Street, designed by Lutyens in 1904

given Tipping the desire to do something more for himself. He must have been envious of Hudson, for whom Deanery Garden had been built between 1899 and 1901 through the joint efforts of Lutyens (house) and Jekyll (gardens); in 1899 he had also guided his old friend Harold Peto (1854–1933; fig.27) in the purchase of Iford Manor and had subsequently seen him design and develop an exceptional garden in the Italian style (fig.28). Mathern Palace was beautiful but limited, and it did not offer much scope for entertaining, especially with his 85-year-old mother there. However, he made a small gesture of independence in 1907 when he bought a piece of land from the St Pierre Estate to develop as a water garden. It was in part an extension of his life at Mathern because the land was only two miles away, but it gave him scope to exercise his skills as a garden designer and it added something new for visitors to see.

27 Harold Peto, photographed at Iford Manor in 1907
28 The Casita at Iford Manor

29

A small stream passed by Mathern, meeting the Severn Estuary at the St Pierre Pill, once an important harbour but now silted up. The stream was called the Mounton Brook and inland, where the Welsh hills began, it cut through a rocky limestone gorge, with sheer cliffs alternating with tree-clad hangers so that the water sometimes surged round a bluff and sometimes ran easily and quietly in the midst of a narrow meadow. From as early as 1750 the gorge had been the site of paper mills, utilising water power to make brown packing paper and paper bags from rope, rags and straw. The 1861 census for the small village of Mounton (fig.29) counts three families of papermakers and in 1871 the three mills were put up for sale as working businesses; the sale advertisement also mentions 'a water corn grist mill, driving three pairs of stones', 'two genteel residences and three workmen's cottages' and 'six acres of capital meadow, pasture and orchard lands'. Not long afterwards the mills were closed following accusations of polluting the water supply, the machinery was sold and production was centralised at the Monmouthshire Board Mills in Newport, so that 30 years later the industrial buildings and most of the homes had been abandoned. It was far from picturesque when Tipping bought the land, probably in 1899, but he could see the potential.

Tipping described the development of the water gardens in his article 'A water garden in the natural style' in *Country Life* for 1 September 1910; much of the same information was repeated in the 2 August 1913 issue of William Robinson's journal *The Garden*. His initial idea was to leave the existing stream banks and surrounding slopes as they were, but heavy rains early in 1908 made him realise that a more radical alteration was necessary. The project then became a work of landscape engineering, using the plentiful supply of local labourers to create an artificial stream-bed where the water could be controlled. He records in his 1908 diary, 'bought railway to help with earth moving' and 'men lay water pipes', and a visit 'to water works where excavating and pipe-laying go merrily'. Tipping ordered a trench 12 ft wide and 5 ft deep to be dug. The surface soil was wheeled away in order that it was not buried but could be used again as topsoil in the new design, while the rockier undersoil was tossed on either bank as unevenly as possible. Irregular side bays were dug out to be used to establish curves, levels and contours that would seem natural. At the bottom of the trench a small waterway was engineered, its windings shaped by realistic bluffs and differing widths created by the placing of barrier stones. Zigzag paths, laid with rough but flattish limestone paving from a neighbouring quarry, led to the water and bordered it (fig.24). His plan shows that the course of the original stream was preserved and water

29 The Mounton Valley, pencil drawing by G.H. Kitchin, 1900
30 (opposite) The stepping stones across the artificial steam in the Mounton water gardens

31

could be let in from the natural to the artificial stream-bed through a pipe in the bank that could be closed, half-closed or opened at will; all this was disguised so that the water appeared to bubble up amid stones as if from a spring. It then moved rapidly over low stone waterfalls and round corners until it reached the wider and more level area, where it could be crossed by stepping stones (fig.30).

The 1910 *Country Life* article (like the many subsequent articles on Mounton for *The Garden*) was not designed to advertise Tipping's own achievement but as an encouragement for other landowners to improve and beautify their estates. Tipping wrote, 'There are considerable areas of much broken and rocky ground encompassing both stream-beds, all of which is planted,' giving details of what he had tried as guidance for his readers (fig.31). He used deciduous trees and tall perennials close to the gorge, lower plants on the rocky piles and lush, large-leaved species along the stream edge with New Zealand flax and Siberian irises added occasionally for height and drama (fig.32).

The plan of the water garden (fig.33) shows a shed set into the boundary wall along the road. This was a storage place for tools but it also incorporated a sleeping platform protected by a considerable overhang for outdoor sleeping which was then in vogue. He noted in his diary on 30 July 1908, 'To Mounton to try sleeping shed – warm foggy night and very pleasant out.' From then on, he regularly walked down to Mounton from Mathern in the evening and in August he wrote, 'Open air sleeping all week.' His friend George Herbert Kitchin drew Tipping sitting outside the sleeping hut in 1909 when he was staying with him (fig.34). There was also a widening of the stream to form a pool and offer the possibility of swimming.

Tipping's 1910 article was a description of the completed water garden, with accompanying photographs, but he had already written about Mounton for *Country Life* in 1908. In the 21 March article, 'Two renovated cottages in Monmouthshire', he enthused about 'the extreme picturesqueness of the limestone gorge . . . which consisted of

31 The stream in springtime

a steep hanging wood, studded with fine indigenous yew trees rising out of the rocky clefts, and of a diminutive flat meadow through which danced the clear stream', but his primary focus was on how to deal with the industrial ruins that still dominated the area. His first instinct was to demolish every sign of previous human habitation, at least on the land he controlled. He noted how 'two of the most neglected cottages constantly caught the eye and spoilt the picture': yet after reflection he decided to restore them in a sympathetic way which suggested the presence of a village, writing that 'the general landscape composition of which they were to form part demanded the retention of the mellow look of age and a perfect simplicity of form'.

The first cottage, named West's, was in sordid condition, with the chimneys collapsing, tiles off or awry, windows broken and the garden full of rubbish and old pots (fig.34). Tipping brought the cottage into the general garden enclosure for the use of a resident gardener, and used the broken walls of the ruined lean-to to make an extension for a comfortable sitting room off the kitchen and a new airy bedroom above. In the original cottage he could not stand upstairs and all the bedrooms opened out of each other. He replaced the ladder staircase with a proper staircase, added a passage going up into the roof space, and raised the windows right up to the roof plate. He obtained old pantiles for the roof and hung the upper storey with elm

32 Rustic bridge with *Clematis montana rubens*

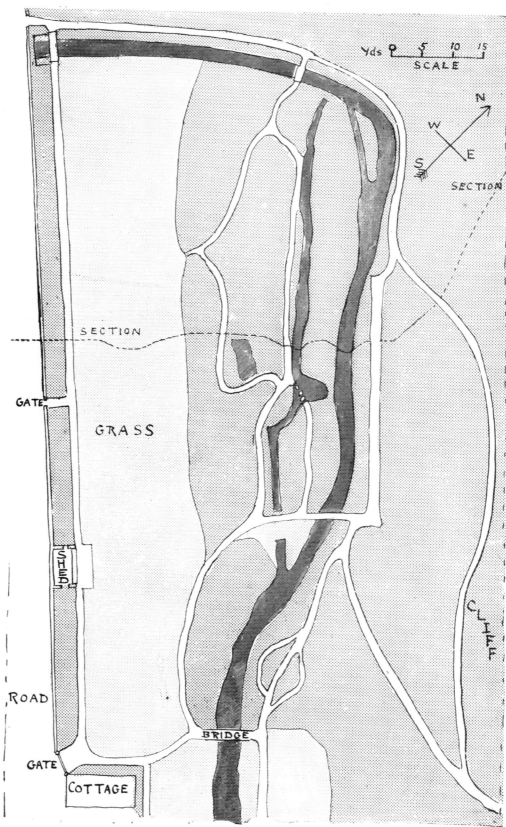

33 Tipping's plan of the water gardens at Mounton, illustrated in *Country Life*, 1910

34

weatherboards (fig.36). The cost of the reconstruction, he recorded, was almost exactly £100.

The other cottage, Jones's, was not needed for staff, so Tipping arranged it 'as holiday quarters for any friend who likes summer picnicking amid beautiful surroundings such as this valley offers', simply improving its appearance and garden. He removed the ruined and leaky roof windows and put new ones in the gable ends. This gave him an unbroken sweep of roof which he brought down over the door, while he added a bay window to add light and sunshine to the living room, where he reopened the old wide hearth and put in fire dogs and a local fire back of 1659 found nearby in the Forest of Dean. He introduced simple oak furniture and an old North Wales livery cupboard (fig.37). In his 1908 diary he describes how he would take visitors on the 2-mile walk from Mathern Palace to have lunch at Jones's and see the water garden. With no added rooms the cost of renovation was £75.

Within five years, in 1913, Tipping was invited to take a seat on the board of the Housing Reform Company at Rhiwbina, a garden village just north of Cardiff. It was built to the plan of Raymond Unwin (1863–1940), who had already worked at New Earswick near York (for the Rowntrees), Letchworth and Hampstead Garden Suburb, and some of the houses were built to Tipping's designs. In 1917 he was asked to supervise a town plan for Chepstow as its population increased to meet a wartime need for shipbuilding; he was disappointed when his appeals for better workers' housing were rejected in favour of cheaper but inferior models. Tipping's interest in social questions, inherited from his Quaker father and mother, is often forgotten but we can say it had its first practical expression in the Mounton gorge.

34 Garden seat and tool shed where Tipping slept on warm nights, pencil sketch by G.H. Kitchin, 1906

35

THE MOUNTON WATER GARDEN

35 West's Cottage before renovation
36 West's Cottage after renovation
37 The living room in Jones's Cottage, where Tipping took his visitors for lunch
38 (overleaf) Entrance front with new topiary and pleached hedging

3. MOUNTON HOUSE

In the 1910 *Country Life* article on the water garden Tipping noted that there was potential for much greater development if the land above and slopes leading down to the gorge were treated as a single unit with what he had already completed:

> The general scheme of the grounds comprised a high and airy tableland, which could adequately accommodate on its comparatively flat surface a house and its terraces. The latter were to be separated by some broken rocky ground set with heaths and low shrubs from the wooded slopes and precipitous sides of the limestone formation, which offered great scope for picturesque wild gardens.

He concludes: 'There was no hurry whatever to realise all this scheme. It was begun ten years ago, and the house and much of the formal lay-out on the upper flat still remain unaccomplished.' There is some uncertainty about the dates when Tipping bought the various pieces of land associated with Mounton but this implies that he had been contemplating a comprehensive plan – house, terraces, rock gardens and pathways down the slopes to reach the water garden – for ten years, and so he must have had an option to buy the land above the gorge in due course. The 1908 diary reveals that he discussed his plans with his friend George Herbert Kitchin at the end of January, even as work on the water garden was under way; in August the railway that had been employed to dig out the stream-bed was re-sited for 'earth work on Mounton hill for terraces' and for the engineering of pathways; on 15 September he wrote 'plan in principle laid down'; and two weeks later he walked Kitchin over the site. In November, 'settle all yews for hedging on new Mounton terraces' – another action which seems to be that of an owner; on 20 December he notes: 'Am now busy for some days trying every possible plan for Mounton new home'; and on Christmas Eve: 'Decide there is nothing so good for Mounton House as old plan with modifications in wings and an attic floor added.'

Thus the design of Mounton House (as it was henceforth called) and the scheme of its surrounding gardens were fully formed in his mind, and even partially laid out, by the end of 1908, but were 'unaccomplished' when he described the water garden in September 1910. The reason for the delay was, surely, that his mother was still alive and too old to be moved from Mathern – and such a grand design was beyond his means, considerable as they were, until he inherited more funds at her death.

All this changed in 1911. Henry's only surviving brother, Colonel William Fearon Tipping, the owner of Brasted Place

39 The flagged terrace above the bowling green

and its associated land and properties, died suddenly and unexpectedly in January of that year, at the age of 64. He had never married and had no children – none of the four brothers had – so Henry found himself as the sole heir of a family fortune worth £271,000, the equivalent of a purchasing power of over £32 million today. Tipping could do all he had imagined, and more, and within a short time he had finalised the purchase of the 60-acre hilltop site at Mounton and the slopes leading to his water garden. One wonders if he told his mother of his grand plans: she was then 89 and with her Quaker background would hardly have approved of such extravagance; but she died in December of the same year, leaving him a smaller but still significant inheritance, and Tipping found himself freed from all moral and financial restraints. He purchased a London house in Dorset Square and set about turning his Monmouthshire dream into reality. It is significant that Tipping's career as full-time architectural editor of *Country Life* from 1907 to 1930 was interrupted in 1910–16 in favour of Lawrence Weaver. He continued to write articles but fewer house visits and trips to London meant that he could dedicate himself to Mounton.

The ten-year gestation period for the Mounton project brought other advantages. Tipping had greatly expanded his knowledge and experience in that time. He had visited and studied many of the great country houses of Britain, writing weekly about their historical aspects and domestic arrangements for *Country Life* magazine, and he could refer to the expertise of Edwin Lutyens and Harold Peto for more detailed and technical information about architecture and construction, while his friends Gertrude Jekyll and William Robinson had helped him develop both academic and practical gardening skills. He had total confidence in his own judgement and taste, which probably explains his choice of architect. Instead of working with someone like Lutyens, who would have had his own firm opinions and was in any case busy with Castle Drogo at the time, Tipping selected Eric Carwardine Francis (1887–1976; fig.40), the son of the Chepstow solicitor who had handled the sale of Mathern. Tipping had been friends with the family for some years, had seen Eric grow up, had no doubt directed his first steps in architecture and was pleased to give him his first major contract – knowing that he would be willing and able to create what was in his client's mind.

Francis was only in his mid-twenties when the Mounton project began, although he was not inexperienced: he had served an apprenticeship under Sir Guy Dawber (1861–1938) and Detmar Blow (1867–1939), both creators of Arts and Crafts manor houses. In time Francis developed his own Arts and Crafts style and his notable works include Wyndcliffe Court (fig.41) and East Cliff (fig.42)

40

near Chepstow, his own home, Long Meadow (fig.43) at West Monkton in Somerset, and Tipping's third and final Monmouthshire home, High Glanau (fig.44). As a local man Eric Francis had good contacts with local builders, craftsmen and suppliers of materials and he proved himself to be an energetic and thoroughly competent project manager; the work on the house and gardens proceeded at an astonishing pace and must have involved an army of specialists and labourers. Construction of Mounton started immediately in 1911, even before the sale of the Tipping properties at Brasted, Masons and bricklayers had completed the structure of the main house by the end of the summer of 1912, so that they could work on the adjunct buildings and garden walls while the interior was finished, and Tipping moved into the house in the late summer of 1913. By May 1914 the first important visitors were arriving at Mounton House.

We know so much about the state of Mounton in these early years because of a major article and photographs in *Country Life*. 'Mounton House, Chepstow, the residence of H. Avray Tipping' appeared in the issue of 15 February 1915, written by Tipping's friend Sir Martin Conway (1856–1937), the explorer and art connoisseur, doubtless under the owner's guidance to make sure that the house was described

40 Eric Carwardine Francis

41

42

43

44

41 Wyndcliffe Court near Chepstow, built by E.C. Francis with garden designed by Tipping
42 Long Meadow, E.C. Francis's own home
43 East Cliff, built for E.C. Francis's brother, 1925
44 High Glanau near Monmouth, Tipping's retirement cottage built by E.C. Francis in 1923

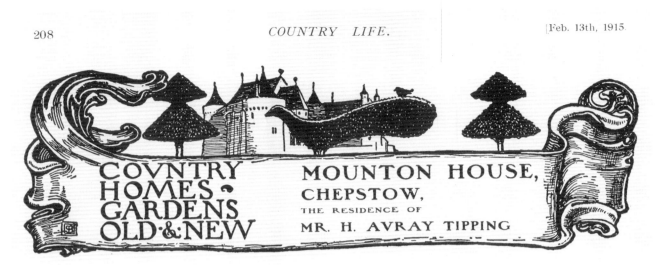

adequately (fig.45). Conway began, 'Readers of *Country Life* are well aware that Mr. Avray Tipping is a knowledgeable person in the matter of English domestic architecture. Many of us have learnt much of what we know on the subject from his articles upon the old houses of England' (indeed, almost 700 had been published by that time). He then continued, 'Today we have to consider him in a new light, as having planned and built *de novo* an imposing house for himself.' He remarks, 'Few architects have had the chance to build so large a house for themselves', and one senses a certain astonishment that a single man, with no immediate family, should launch into such a grand project without any apparent considerations of expense or practicality: 'The designer has had a free hand, and has built what he pleased for himself.'

Clive Aslet, a successor of Tipping as architectural editor of *Country Life* in the 1980s and editor in the 1990s, has written about the houses built in the period 1890–1939 in his book *The Last Country Houses* (1982) and has distinguished two main types, the social and the romantic. The social were the great mansions built without any regard for setting, luxurious to the point of vulgarity and designed to attract important guests and so promote the social advancement of their owners. Romantic houses might also be large but were more likely to be lived in all year and were more at home in their landscapes, using local materials as advocated by the Arts and Crafts movement. Mounton House is a hybrid of these two types. Its main rooms were designed for entertainment – and among the first guests was David Lloyd George, then Chancellor of the Exchequer (although he, like Tipping, was an outsider in the world of the aristocracy). Yet Tipping's choice of the Welsh hills, his personal attention to the gardens, and his preference for local stone

and wood in the construction mark it clearly as a romantic house. In addition Mounton had a third purpose, which is perhaps unique: in continuity with his work at *Country Life*, Tipping wanted the house to provide an education in taste. Within the harmonious outer shell, each room was different, demonstrating the architectural features and furnishings of different periods, and often reproducing details of historic rooms he had seen on his travels. It was a 'show house', certainly, but unlike mansions such as Bryanston (1889–94) or Skibo Castle (1899), Mounton was not designed principally to impress but to teach.

The site of the house was 'a plateau sloping gently towards the south-west and commanding fine views over the Bristol Channel to the distant Mendips'. Tipping similarly designed a house to make the best of a view at High Glanau, and it was what he lacked at Mathern Palace, although the exposure also brought disadvantages, as Conway notes:

> The actual site was a bare, treeless field, widely visible. Hence the buildings ran the risk of great

45 Mounton House, title page from an article in *Country Life*, February 1915
46 Gardeners' cottages and drive

prominence, and might have looked from afar for years like a packing case thrown down in the field. It was also to stand exposed to mighty gales sweeping in from the Atlantic.

Tipping himself completely understood the problems and worked out a design with Francis which turned them into opportunities. There was 'openness to the south-west sun and view', with large windows on that side of the house, while the long bulk of the house itself and numerous associated walls and outbuildings protected the terrace and formal gardens to provide 'the comfortable twin feeling of shelter and seclusion'.

The orientation of the house to exploit the view meant that it did not have a grand entrance; rather, the approach was between buttressed walls and the gable ends of domestic outbuildings (fig.46) – as suggested by the layout of barns at Markenfield Hall, Yorkshire, a late medieval house that Tipping wrote about in *Country Life* in 1912. The walls concealed the parterre garden on the house side and the kitchen garden opposite, and then the kitchen court and laundry respectively. All these buildings were in the same style as the house but in a simpler form, avoiding untidiness by the use of enclosed courtyards which could be planted out. The approach ended in a colonnade where a right-angled turn led into the forecourt of the house (fig.47).

The forecourt was enclosed by a low stone wall in front and a higher one on the left, shutting off the kitchen yards. On the right a long single-storey building held the gallery, with its own entrance so that guests for receptions could be received directly without entering the main house. The outer surface of the house was (and is) harmonious both with the surroundings and in itself, in the best Arts and Crafts style, disguising the creativity and eclecticism of the rooms within. The limestone used for building work was quarried on the estate and is dashed with pinks, purples and other warm and varied tones. The entrance facade (facing north) is defined by a short gabled wing on each side with a contrasting close-spaced half-timbering of the central porch and front door 'emphasised by a slight projection carried upwards above the main level of the eaves' (fig.48). This juxtaposition of materials was similar to Brinsop Court (fig.49) in Herefordshire, a late medieval house where Tipping had recently advised on the restoration. As Conway wrote, 'the general effect is plain but agreeable', with the only other outstanding feature being the chimneys, all of them on interior

47 East of the forecourt drive, pencil drawing by G.H. Kitchin, 19 May 1917
48 (overleaf) Entrance front

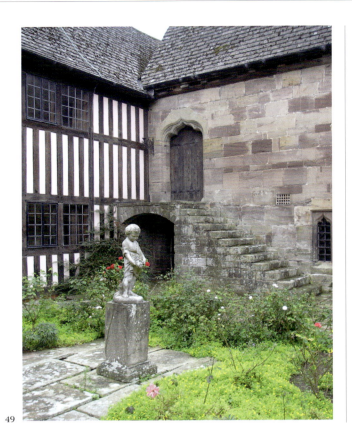

walls so as not to waste the heat of the fires. Although roofs in Monmouthshire were often made of local stone tiles, at Mounton the tiles were brought from further away, while local oak was used for the windows (fig.51).

The south front (fig.52), facing the sunshine, the garden and the view, is long and framed by three gables, the two end projections forming loggias, the west one open and the east with round-headed French windows. The paved terrace extends the full length of the garden side and is warm and well sheltered, the gables and coped walls at either end providing the sense of a series of protected outdoor rooms, with one designated for summer dining. The upper storey between the projections was hung with green Westmorland slates. Tipping added dated lead-pipe heads with the Tipping coat of arms and crest (fig.53). These may have been made by Messrs Henry Hope & Sons and been recommended by his colleague Lawrence Weaver, who published a book on English leadwork in 1909.

The considerable kitchens and servants' quarters were on the eastern side, set back from the terrace and hidden from the forecourt by a high wall. They were well planned, with a service area next to the dining room, a pantry and larder off the spacious kitchen, and even their own indoor

49 Half-timbering at Brinsop Court; a new wing was added by Tipping in 1911
50 Ground floor plan, Mounton House
51 (opposite) Watercolour of the north-west angle of the Courtyard (at Brinsop Court) by Gwen Dorrien-Smith in 1921

52 The garden facade

MOUNTON HOUSE

53 Lead pipe head with date and Tipping family crest

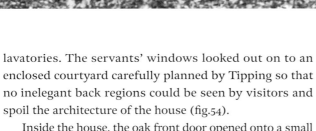

54 The kitchen court

lavatories. The servants' windows looked out on to an enclosed courtyard carefully planned by Tipping so that no inelegant back regions could be seen by visitors and spoil the architecture of the house (fig.54).

Inside the house, the oak front door opened onto a small lobby, beyond which was a square hall in the medieval style from which ascended the main staircase (fig.55), copied from Park Hall in Shropshire, and with doors leading to the two great downstairs rooms of the main house. Each of them faced towards the gardens and the view, and each had long walls on that side pierced by three windows and framed by the gables of the south facade. To the east, on the side of the kitchens, is the dining room (fig.56), and here, after the rather dark entrance to the house, the liberty of Tipping's conception immediately became apparent. Any hint of the medieval or Elizabethan disappeared because the dining room was entirely decorated and furnished in the style of the late 18th century. The door cases and mottled grey and white marbled chimneypiece were built by Robert Adam in 1784 and brought from Brasted Place in Kent, Tipping's family home. Two round-headed china cabinets were built into the long wall, facing the three windows, to house Tipping's collection of faience, and there were delicate plaster wreaths on ceiling and walls. The floor was marble but could be carpeted for warmth in winter, and there was an associated loggia at the south-east corner with large sliding glass doors that could be thrown open to the sun and air. As Conway notes, the light and open style was 'particularly suited to a dining room, as napery, silver, glass and china look well in such surroundings'.

Balancing this room, to the west and in a completely different style (of the first third of the 17th century), was the great parlour, some 38 ft in length and panelled in oak in heavy Jacobean style (fig.56). It was similar to the room

55 Staircase copied from Park Hall in Shropshire
56 (overleaf) The great parlour

from the Old Palace at Bromley-by-Bow, first displayed at the Victoria and Albert Museum in 1894, which Tipping helped to buy for the nation, and the moulded plaster ceiling, with broad enriched relief bands forming complex patterns, was a copy of the ceiling of 1610–11 in Prince Henry's Room over the Inner Temple Gateway in London, the centre of which displays the Prince of Wales feathers and initials P.H. (fig.59). Guests would not have been aware of it, but with this room Tipping and Francis demonstrated their willingness to use the most modern methods to create a historical effect: the huge moulded plaster ceiling was supported by a concrete floor above. Significantly, the first reinforced concrete building in Europe was just 65 miles away in Swansea; known as the Victoria Flour Mills or Weaver's Flour Mill, it was opened in 1898 and designed by the French engineer François Hennebique (1842–1921); they may also have been aware of the extensive use of concrete in the new Avonmouth Docks (1902–1908) and the first English reinforced-concrete rail bridge at Bristol, designed in 1907 by L.G. Mouchel, the UK agents for the Hennebique system. Tipping's surprising choice of ferro-concrete for Mounton, although completely hidden, may be the first large-scale use of the material in a domestic setting. Conway's article noted another novelty: 'The lighting here, as elsewhere throughout the house, is by electricity, and the central lamps in this room are hung, in two circles each of eight lights, from

57 Dining room in the Adam style

a wooden ring or crown.' He remarks that the lighting is effective and adds, 'It is easy to guess that this clever invention is likely to be widely imitated' – although by 1919 only 6 per cent of British homes were wired up. The full-height Doric columns and pilasters which incorporated the great fireplace on the far wall had their counterparts forming a pseudo-screen framing the two doors on the entrance wall. Tipping's furniture, also Jacobean, included three carved court cupboards on one side facing the three windows, a long refectory table in the middle and other smaller tables, chairs and cabinets – 'not all English' but 'all old and enviable'. Conway is obviously speaking from personal experience when he writes: 'It is, to my thinking, the most attractive of all the nice rooms in the house, a thoroughly liveable place, where you can read or talk round the ample tea table before the large log fire, or take your ease according to your mood.'

Beyond the great parlour, in the western gable, were Tipping's library (fig.60) and study (called the work room on the Ground Floor Plan). The library was panelled in oak and led into the west loggia and garden, while the work room (fig.61), with windows to the forecourt and more bookshelves, was dominated by an inventive Arts and Crafts brick fireplace designed by Francis, utilising special 1-inch bricks in the Italian style and incorporating cast reliefs of terracotta. Tipping later copied this fireplace when he advised on a new wing at Weston Hall in Herefordshire.

The dining room was separated from the great parlour (which is a very masculine room) by a small ladies' sitting room (fig.61) occupying the central projection on the south front and flooded with light from three large windows overlooking the terrace to east, south and west. There was a marble fireplace, surmounted by a carved mantelpiece of about 1720, and the furniture and decorations were chosen to correspond to that date – 'English satinwood or French Louis XVI, all genuine'. Being relatively small, and with its exceptional view of the garden, it is probable that Tipping used this sitting room when he was on his own.

The third great room of Mounton was accessible from his work room (fig.62) but was essentially separate from the structure of the main house: the single-storey gallery (fig.63) which occupied the whole of the west side of the forecourt. Conway remarks that the separation meant that 'if in days to come great revelry goes on there, it will not disturb either the studious in the library or the weary in the bedrooms'. Again it was a well-lit room, in its own distinctive style designed to house a collection of French furniture purchased

58 Advertisement in *Country Life* showing the great parlour ceiling at Mounton, 1915
59 Plasterwork ceiling in the great parlour showing Prince Henry's initials

60

61

by Tipping's parents, the largest pieces being three 18th-century Normandy armoires. Sadly the hoped-for revelry was muted by the time Conway wrote in 1915.

Nor was the upstairs, with its 12 bedrooms and six bathrooms, fully used by house guests (whose accompanying lady's maids or valets could be housed in the attic). Conway writes that the bedrooms were 'all lofty (owing to the high roof), sunny, and commanding the entrancing view', but there must have been only one or two occupants, old friends, for much of the war. Tipping's own bedroom (fig.64) was unique, occupying the south-west corner of the house and 'a bedroom counterpart in style to the great parlour below'. It was divided into two parts, separated by an open balustraded screen: the entrance lobby had a flat ceiling while the inner part, the bedroom proper, was higher with a decorated plasterwork wagon ceiling of Jacobean type, copied from the gallery ceiling at Chastleton, Oxfordshire. Tipping added the family coat of arms and the date of the house in the plasterwork on the north side of the wagon ceiling and his own initials and crest on the south (fig.65). Tipping had recently restored a similar screen at Brinsop Court. The furniture, including a solid four-poster bed, was all oak and of the same period as the pieces in the parlour.

The total cost of Mounton House (the house alone) was £40,000, just under £5 million at current values. In many ways the interior of Mounton could be said to be old-fashioned – although in fact it demonstrated the fashions of several past centuries – but it was both functional and highly imaginative, and the varied interiors show real craftsmanship. Doubtless Tipping was influenced by houses he had recently visited and by friends and colleagues, but he alone was, as Sir Martin Conway calls him, 'the creator of all these spacious and dignified surroundings', the polymath who both designed everything and brought the work to completion in less than three years.

60 The Library
61 Ladies' sitting room
62 (opposite) Work room with Arts and Crafts fireplace designed by Eric Francis
63 (overleaf) The long gallery, a single-storey wing for entertaining

64 (opposite) Tipping's bedroom
65 Bedroom plasterwork showing Tipping's initials and crest
66 (overleaf) Garden facade from the rock garden

4. THE GARDENS OF MOUNTON HOUSE

We have a wealth of information about the development of the gardens at Mounton. Tipping himself wrote the *Country Life* article on them for 28 July 1917, using photographs taken in the summer of 1916, by which time most of the plantings had sufficiently matured, although he noted that with so many men called to battle certain areas had become overgrown or neglected. He entrusted the garden photographs to A.E. Henson, who the next year began 40 years with *Country Life* as a full-time photographer. Some were taken at the end of June when wind and rain apparently made things difficult and others in early August. Henson's diary of those visits gives an insight into the social distinctions that prevailed even in wartime. Although Tipping had a dozen empty bedrooms and knew Henson well from years of collaboration, the photographer stayed at Skyrme's boarding house in Chepstow (fig.68) and in the evening was given 'supper' – presumably in the Mounton servants' hall – rather than dinner at the owner's table. Tipping later reworked the 1917 article for a chapter in his 1925 book *English Gardens* and in both he reflects on the difficulty of starting a garden next to a building site. In 1917 he writes: 'Builders encompass their objective with an area almost as catastrophic... as a Picardy homestead abandoned by retreating Huns.' In 1925 this becomes 'as catastrophic as an earthquaked Tokio (*sic*)', referring to the Great Kanto Earthquake of 1923 in which Frank Lloyd Wright's Imperial Hotel was one of the few buildings to survive.

These two general views of the design of the gardens are supplemented by an extraordinarily detailed series of articles for *The Garden*, the journal professional gardeners were more likely to read. Tipping had already written about the water garden for them in 1913; now he produced 11 further articles on Mounton, three in 1916, four in 1917, and two each in 1920 and 1921. They touch on the construction of walls and rock gardens, the choice of plants for different conditions, the vagaries of the British weather and the delights (and sometimes disappointments) of the seasons, and they reveal Tipping as not just a designer but also a passionate and knowledgeable practical gardener.

His friends William Robinson and Gertrude Jekyll had both served as editors of *The Garden* and in places he shows the profound influence they had had on his thought and on his hands-on approach to gardening. They had been the catalysts for a major change in the design of the English garden from the formal parterres and garish bedding out so popular in the high Victorian age to a preference for gardens as part of the natural landscape. They understood that this meant a compromise, and Tipping concurred: 'The old school of formalists aimed at

67 Rectangular lily pool with water-spouting boy, 1920

banishing Nature, just as the late landscapists sought to banish formalism. Our best schools of to-day ... rightly insist upon combining the two.' In the diverse settings and microclimates of Mounton Tipping drew on his knowledge of plants and was prepared to experiment, introducing new varieties and operating a policy of survival of the fittest. In the 1917 *Country Life* article he comments:

> Against the house were set a variety of climbers and wall shrubs, all of which did well till last winter taught them the rigours of life. *Cilanthus puniceus* was done to death ... Of veronicas all the speciose hybrids succumbed, but *Hulkeana* survived, although reckoned a somewhat tender subject.

Tipping wrote in his diary on 9 September 1912 (nine months after the death of his mother) of 'pavement laying and other garden work in progress', followed six weeks later by the entry, 'pergola garden being planted and dry wall beginning'. This period saw the inception of most of the formal garden at Mounton House, although the yew hedges and the construction of the rocky bank and the bowling green below had been started as early as 1908. The gardens are composed of three separate regions: the natural wood and water garden created in the limestone gorge far below the house; the contrasting formal garden around Tipping's house on the plateau above with its terraces, pergola and walled areas, including a broad flight of steps leading down to the bowling green which was surrounded by clipped yew hedging; and the less formal rock garden, shrub banks and tree plantings which stood between the two and provided a transition: Q, O and P on the sketch plan of the garden made for his 1925 book *English Gardens* (fig.69).

For Tipping's visitors, the gardens began with the flagged terrace next to the house (fig.70). In between the projecting gables there were sheltered paved areas for sitting out on windy days and at each end of the terrace protruding coped walls, pierced by arched doorways, gave a further feeling of shelter and seclusion, the doorways giving enticing views to what lay beyond: the pergola garden and dining loggia to the south-east (figs 71 and 72) and the steep precipice to the gorge to the north-west (fig.73). Within the most sheltered area of the terrace Tipping tried pomegranates and myrtles, magnolias and Edwardsias and *Solanum jasminoides* and *Solanum crispum* to climb the house walls – although with varying success because of winter storms, as we have seen. In the retaining wall bays *Carpenteria californica* flowered profusely and against the pillars that start from the bowling-green level he planted the strongest of rambling roses, American Pillar (fig.74). At either end of the bowling green,

68 Chepstow High street, showing Skyrme's Cafe where A.E. Henson stayed when photographing Mounton for *Country Life*

THE GARDENS OF MOUNTON HOUSE

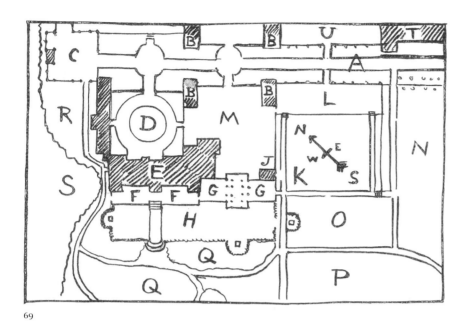

A. the drive between buttressed walls
B. gable ends of garage and outbuildings
C. colonnade
D. forecourt
E. house
F. terrace
G. pergola garden
H. bowling green
I. tea house
J. lawn
K. parterre
L. kitchen court and rose garden
M. tennis court
N. shrub bank
O. tree-planted rough ground
P. rock garden
Q. west garden
R. precipitious descent to water garden
S. cottages
T. kitchen garden

69 Plan of house and formal gardens
70 The terrace looking east

in front of a circle of yew, Tipping set the huge urns that he brought from Brasted Place (fig.75), and to the south there was a statue of the goddess Diana, precisely placed opposite the end of the pergola (fig.76).

Through the doorway at the south-eastern end of the terrace there were three steps down into the pergola garden that stretched beyond the house (fig.77). Tipping wrote about the planting of the area closest to the house in his article on tulips for *The Garden* in 1916:

> The object is to have a show in May, and therefore only late tulips are used in these sections of the grounds. The site being high and open, stiff stems are desirable, and chief reliance is placed on the Darwin group. Some thousand being needed and cost an object, the best of the older varieties are selected, but among them Clare Butt, now supplied at 40s. per thousand, is now happily included.

71 South-east court and dining loggia in spring
72 The pergola garden in tulip-time

73 North-west court and open loggia
74 The pergola bay, showing American Pillar rose on the pergola above the bowling green

75

76

77

Feb. 20th, 1915.]   COUNTRY LIFE.   233

IN THE GARDEN.

IN THE GARDEN AT MOUNTON HOUSE.

ALTHOUGH Mounton House, the subject of last week's "Country Home," was only recently completed, the portion of its grounds that occupies a limestone gorge is quite a dozen years old, and was described in an illustrated article in COUNTRY LIFE on September 10th, 1910. Since then it has still further matured, and when our photographer revisited it last August it presented a scene of peaceful luxuriance, in strong contrast to the gardens of our Allies, the Belgians, already devastated by a ruthless invader. The picture now given represents a group of the giant Meadow-sweet, with the wooded cliff behind it. It is set near enough to the babbling brook to profit by the dampness and sends up strong but numerous shoots, which call for liberal thinning so that the survivors may rise to a height of 8ft. or more, and be of such stoutness that they will withstand the wind without any support, and thus retain to the full their natural gracefulness. Just showing on the left-hand side is an outlier of a colony of Fleabane, whose lance-like stems and flower-heads contrast pleasantly with the broad leaves and flattish heads of the Spiræa, while they rise from a golden bed of dwarf Helenium. Thus a good late summer effect is produced, replacing an earlier display of Crane's-bills, Columbines and other June flowerers.

The second picture shows a quite different gardening aspect, for, as the house on its open tableland is approached, Nature gives way to formalism, geometric beds replace natural planting and high walls are substituted for rocky tree-clad banks. Some of the terraces appear in the house pictures, but the less architectural parterre is shown with this article, together with

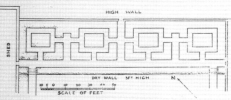

PLAN OF PARTERRE.

GIANT MEADOW-SWEET IN THE WILD GARDEN.

its plan. It occupies a space about 170ft. long by 45ft. wide. Facing south-west it is raised, by means of an Alpine-clad dry wall, 3ft. above the croquet lawn, and overlooks the fertile flats by Severn's side, the silver streak of the estuary itself and the Somerset hills beyond. On all other sides it is protected by wall and building, so that though south-westers, arriving straight from the Atlantic, dictate the choice of dwarf-growing plants, except near the walls, the more tender subjects do not suffer from Boreas' icy blasts. The parterre is composed of broad ways laid with self-faced Yorkshire paving, and of ample-sized beds and borders. The plan is of great simplicity. This is a place for flowering plants, and the whole effect is to be produced by them. The setting is to show them off, not to assert itself and vie with them. Against the walls are placed, together with Wistarias and climbing Roses, somewhat delicate shrubs, such as Crinodendron Hookeri and Olearia macrocephala, Feijoa sellowiana and Teucrium latifolium, Illicium floridanum and anisatum, Escallonia revoluta and pterocladum. These are still in a young state, and few as yet peer above the seven foot high Golden Rods and Heleniums that stand in the borders before them at the ends of the parterre devoted to reds and yellows, or the tall Larkspurs and Asters that occupy a like position in the central region, where blues and pinks predominate.

The four large oblong beds are each set with 100 Dwarf Polyantha Roses, of which Orleans and Mrs. Cutbush have proved the most satisfactory, both in vigour of growth and persistence of flowering. Lavender Violas edge and fill all gaps in these Rose colonies. The L-shaped beds placed in front of the oblongs are what show best in the picture. The early display of Delphinium Persimmon and Mrs. Thompson, both dwarf growers of fine form and colour, of pink Pæonies and Sweet Williams, of blue Irises and rose Helianthemums is over, and their place is

taken by Sedum spectabile, Eryngiums alpinum and oliverianum, Scabious and Aster Thomsoni. Why is this Aster not more used? At Mounton House and at the owner's other garden at Mathern Palace we find it, in different aspects, flourishing by the dozen and even hundred. No Michaelmas Daisy has a

THE PAVED PARTERRE: LOOKING S.W. OVER BRISTOL CHANNEL AND MENDIPS.

pleasanter blue or more shapely flower. It is dwarf and holds itself up admirably. Its flower season lasts from the end of July till the beginning of October. It occupies little space while early bloomers hold sway, but lightly arches its flowering stems over their remnants later on. It is not difficult to grow, its only bad trick being to rot away in winter. But this it seldom does after withstanding one year, and not at all if the position is open and the soil fairly light and well drained. In the red and yellow end regions, the corresponding beds are liberally set with Geum Mrs. Bradshaw and Potentilla Gibson's Scarlet, both of which have an exceptionally vigorous habit and long blooming season. Gaillardias and Coreopsis, Kniphofias and Pentstemons add their quota to the wealth of flower. On the other side of the long 6ft. wide paved way is a narrow border, influenced by the alpine

---

75 The Brasted urns brought from Tipping's family home
76 Diana statue bought from the Duke of Sutherland's sale at Trentham, Staffordshire
77 Darwin tulips in the pergola garden, autochrome by Reginald Malby, 1920
78 Article by Tipping in *Country Life*: 'In the Garden at Mounton House'

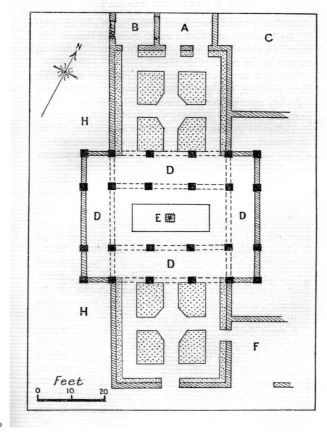

80

A rectangular lily pool occupied the centre of the stone pergola, which comprised an astonishing 24 pillars, and in the centre of the pool stood a water-spouting boy on a column surrounded by water lilies (fig.67). This statue, a copy from Pompeii and not of the *Manneken Pis* of Brussels, is exactly the same as the one in the pool on the garden front at Deanery Garden. The pergola was planted with roses and wisteria. Tipping commented on one of the photographs in the 1917 article in *Country Life* that 'the parapet wall that runs along the open side of the pergola garden is seen altogether bosomed with Dorothy Perkins and Lady Gay, which at this height escape mildew and grow riotously'. The surrounding formal beds where 'tall Darwin tulips sway in the wind' in May 'are mauve with Maggie Mott violas' later in the summer. Tipping considered the pergola garden (fig.79) a tribute to William Robinson, whom he called 'our horticultural doyen, the senior alderman of our gardening corporation'. Gertrude Jekyll was impressed by the Mounton pergola, using it as an illustration in her book *Garden Ornament* (1918). She noted, 'Mr Avray Tipping's pergola at Mounton or Mr Robinson's structures at Gravetye depend for their effect on a luxuriant overgrowth' (see p.2). It was also similar to the pergola designed by Harold Peto at the Villa Rosemary in the Alpes-Maritimes in 1910–11, which Tipping wrote about for *Country Life* in 1912. Tipping was clearly proud of the pergola and drew a plan of it (fig.80) in his book *The Garden of To-day* (1933). He described it as:

> opening from the dining-loggia (A) with arches opening west on to a terrace (B) but south into a privy garden with three sides enclosed by buildings or high walls, the fourth or west side being a parapeted terrace wall raising the little garden up from the lawn (H) and giving a wide prospect. The pergola (D) occupies the central portion, its length being the breadth of the privy garden increased by bays. The western bay stretches out into the lawn from which, there being four feet of retaining wall, the pergola piers rise fourteen feet. From the level of the privy garden they rise ten feet, by no means too much to sustain the rafter arrangement on which the rambler roses and Japanese wisterias lie. Supported by the ten foot east wall the pergola forms a sort of open cloister with paved walks and flower-beds on each side of it, while the centre is shaped as a broad paved area framing an oblong pool (E).

79 (opposite) Central alley of the pergola garden
80 Pergola plan from Tipping's *The Garden of To-day* (1933)

81

82

From the pergola garden it was possible to pass out to the croquet lawn, either through the door or through an open-sided two-storey tea house (fig.81). It was surrounded by tall stone walls, once again for shelter, and Lady Congreve remembered being shown around this part of the garden with her husband: '"That wall must have cost you a pretty penny, Harry," said my husband. "Yes," said Harry in his most incisive way. "You see, I do not care to keep racehorses or dancing ladies. I prefer to spend my money on walls."' (Celia Congreve, 11 years younger than Tipping, had known him since her childhood at Brasted and was one of the few people who felt able to tease him).

Above the lawn there was what Tipping called the parterre, a paved area with inset flowerbeds where there was a June show of peonies and, later in the season, a display of *Aster thomsonii*, one of Tipping's favourite flowers. He used great drifts of the same flower, in the way advocated by Jekyll, to soften the geometric stonework in several places (fig.82). In 1912 Tipping was commissioned by Lord Lee to lay out a new walled garden at Chequers similar to the parterre at Mounton (fig.84). The tea house was 'a garden

---

81   The tea house and environing walls
82   Flower border in the parterre garden
83   (opposite) Two-storey tea house with shady sitting area below and sleeping room above
84   (overleaf) The paved garden that Tipping designed for Lord Lee at Chequers in 1912

85

86

85 Looking down the west garden on the edge of the gorge
86 Looking up the west garden to the colonnade with statue of *The Grape Picker* by Francisque Joseph Duret
87 (opposite) The colonnaded garden, autochrome by Reginald Malby, 1920

house overlooking the croquet lawn, which, facing east, provides a shady sitting-room below and sleeping-out loggia above'(fig.83). To the west of the house, on the edge of the gorge, there was a colonnaded garden (R on the plan) with statues overlooking the unspoilt valley below (fig.85); the statue of *The Grape Picker* by Francisque Joseph Duret was a copy from the Louvre (fig.86). Again this was filled with Darwin tulips in springtime, as shown in contemporary photographs (fig.87).

In the area between the formal gardens and the wild water garden Tipping created a rock garden to the south-west where there had been a stone quarry (fig.88). Where the quarrying had been deepest Tipping made pools: the hollows were increased and then cemented, incorporating pudlo into the mix, and as an extra precaution two coats of tar were applied, sanded over to ensure there were no leaks. The central part was left for water, and the irregular margins were bordered with rocks suitable for dry-loving alpines. *Primula pulverulenta*, *Primula rosea*, *Cypripedium spectabile* and *Astilbes* all thrived here. To the south-east were shrubs and trees, concealing the presence of a tennis court, yet another occasion of recreation for his guests. Further below there were viewing platforms and winding paths (fig.90) among the natural rock formations (fig.91) to reach the bottom of the valley and Tipping's water garden. This area of semi-natural woodland was planted with mixed deciduous and coniferous trees.

The garden at Mounton was certainly a testament to Tipping as designer and plantsman, with every detail carefully pondered and executed (fig.89). It is a garden of strong structural bones, softened and relaxed by luxuriant plantings.

87

ROCK GARDENING AT MOUNTON HOUSE

By H. Avray Tipping, M.A.

THE gardens surrounding Mounton House occupy some acres of slightly sloping table-land and a section of a limestone gorge that edges the table-land on the south and west. A large part of the former area is laid out formally, while the whole of the latter is given over to the wild and water gardens. There is, however, an interspace—a fringe of the arable field that used to occupy the table-land, of which the unevenness has been intensified, especially where quarrying operations were carried on, and the rocky character revealed. This ex-quarry forms the foreground of the illustration, two terraces—the one grass, the other paved—lying between it and the house. Where the quarrying had been deepest, pools were made. The hollow was increased and then cemented. Although pudlo was added to the cement, the extra precaution was taken of giving two coats of hot tar, sanded over, as a leak after completion would have been disastrous. Only the central portion of the cemented area was left for the water, a considerable but very irregular margin being bordered with rocks and filled in behind them with sandy and peaty earth, forming a morass, whence the moisture, by capillary action, is in a measure transmitted to the soil beyond the cemented area. Thus, in a very open and sunny spot, subjects needing much or moderate moisture are accommodated without the necessity of watering, while the rocky banks around are well suited to many a dry-loving alpine, with water at need from a handy hose-pipe, supplied, as are the pools, from the estate water main. The tall flowering stems of Primula pulverulenta and the elegant leaves of Rodgersia podophylla are seen by the waterside in the foreground of the picture, reproduced from a photograph taken last May. Earlier in the spring the sturdy stems of Caltha polypetala had carried the heads of golden bloom above the big leaves, the whole jutting out into the water and reflected therein. The stateliness of these plants is enhanced by making them rise out of an undergrowth of Primula rosea and Omphalodes verna blooming at the same time. Then follows a selection of the tall Primroses of the japonica type, of which Bees' hybrids give much variety of tone. That enterprising nursery also offers excellent Mimuluses (of which the dwarf, vivid-coloured Whitecroft Scarlet is perhaps the gem) that begin to bloom as the Primulas go off and before Astilbes begin. Of the latter it is the pink ones, such as Ceres and Salmon Queen, that find a home here. Cypripedium spectabile and Iris Kæmpferi flourish in the marsh; while in the damp soil just beyond it is a happy colony of Columbines of the cærulea type strengthened by crossing with a more vigorous breed without loss of the long spurs. Rising from the marsh is a rocky mound wherein a group of Ramondia pyrenaica is set vertically, facing north and additionally shaded as summer progresses by the foliage of the tall Astilbe Davidii. Next to it, but having more sun and light, its cousin Haberlea rhodopensis so crowds its allotted chinks that it needs frequent thinning. Beyond the humid area many Campanulas, such as Raineri, pulla and G. F. Wilson, have spread so as to assume the look of natural patches. Various Saxifrages, Dianthi and Stonecrop clothe the ground, and the sunniest spots are given to alpine Wallflowers, Æthionemas and Linums, all of which have suffered badly this winter, as also have certain shrubs associated with them, such as Cistuses and Veronicas, Fuchsias and Coronilla glauca. Many, I hope, will recover, but they are needing drastic cutting back and will be poor-looking things at best during this season, which promises to be one of sufficient gloom through the action of the Hun without any ugly knock on the part of Dame Nature. Luckily, the injured innocents occupy only a fraction of the ground. The broken rock-strewn stretch beyond the pools and their banks shows much herbaceous stuff in bloom, of which Irises are most conspicuous in the photograph, and beyond them shrubs, among which groups of white Portugal Broom and of Exochorda macrantha are covered with flower. I never succeeded in making Exochorda grandiflora quite at home here. The lime in the soil makes its foliage poor and yellowish, and there is not the vigour needed for a fine display of bloom. But its descendant, the macrantha variety, I tried as soon as it was introduced, and it does excellently. I have bushes 8 feet high and as much across, producing yearly an abundance of bloom-buds which, unfortunately, are liked by the birds, so that the fulfilment of flower is apt not to be quite equal to the promise. Where the photograph ends on the left there is an open, undulating area set with hundreds of plants of Erica carnea and its offspring Erica mediterranea hybrida (syn. E. darleyensis, Bean). They often show flowering sprigs before Christmas, and are rich in colour during February. Not so this cold winter, but the frost has had no ill effect beyond delay, and these early days of April are made bright by their sheet of bloom. In the background, but occasionally coming forward among the Heaths, are flowering shrubs, Lilacs and Deutzias, Forsythias and Rhus Cotinus purpureus. The latter covers itself with crimson purple fluff as July opens, and, even when the colour dies out into grey as autumn advances, it remains a source of joy, for its foliage assumes rich tints. In the more rocky section to the right of the main path, dwarf growths occupy the foreground. Stony flats to walk on get carpeted with Woolly Thyme. With a little care and frequent resowing of collected seed the beautiful Linaria alpina—both the type and the rosy variety—is kept going on the edge of the gravel. Type Violas, especially gracilis, are encouraged to spread. The rosy Gypsophila and the Maiden Pink embrace each other as they spread. Behind stretches of Creeping Phlox are tufts of the Canadian species as improved by Mr. Perry. It is apt to disappear entirely after a most successful season, but is easily propagated by breaking up a few plants every summer, and is a subject well worth much more pains and trouble than that. For a long period in the late spring its numerous stems are topped with a perfect cluster of pale blue flowers in the manner well shown in the illustration. These plants continued for three seasons without

A ROCK GARDEN IN A QUARRY.

---

88 (opposite) Steep rock garden
89 Article in *The Garden* written by Tipping in 1917: 'Rock Gardening at Mounton House'

90 Path winding down to the water gardens below the rock garden

91 Rocks in the hanger
92 (overleaf) Rock garden with specimen trees

5. FROM HIGH SUMMER TO WARTIME

By May 1914 Mounton was ready to receive guests. Construction was finished, not least the complex craftsmanship of interior plasterwork and panelling; major pieces of furniture and garden statuary had been brought from Brasted Place; staff had been recruited, including 12 'outside staff', of whom ten were gardeners; and, although it was still early in the growing season, the garden had a show of Darwin tulips. Colleagues and acquaintances from *Country Life* would have been early visitors, among them Home Gordon, 12th Baronet Gordon of Embo, who was a prolific cricket writer. His wife Lady Edith Gordon recorded in her memoir *The Winds of Time*: 'In the spring of 1914 we went to stay with Mr Avray Tipping in his lovely new house at Chepstow, with marvellous gardens of many delights. Lloyd George (fig.94) and a large party of Welsh members, their wives and families came over on Sunday for lunch. I sat next him and we talked of Ulster, which of course was the one subject of conversation.' Lady Gordon was a Kerry native who just the year before had built an Arts and Crafts house, Ard na Sighe, on Caragh Lake and was passionately concerned about Irish Home Rule. This kind of gathering of the politically informed, with the social cachet of entertaining the Chancellor of the Exchequer, was just what Tipping had hoped for. He was also prepared to show the house to more humble guests, such as the Aberdare Gardeners and Allotment Holders' Society who came in the first week of July; Tipping himself led them through the house while Mr Spencer, the head gardener, gave them a tour of the grounds and gardens. One wonders how aware they were that their lives were about to change: the assassination of Archduke Franz Ferdinand on 28 June and the subsequent 'July Crisis' led inexorably to Britain's entry into war on 4 August.

There was the initial hope that the war would be swift, a war of movement that would be 'over by Christmas', more or less like the Franco-Prussian War of 1870–1. Perhaps that is why Sir Martin Conway's February 1915 article for *Country Life* reflected nothing of war conditions. He imagined Tipping looking out to east, to south and to west from his bedroom windows and surveying his work:

> To the left his eyes can enfilade the south front of the house and the terrace below it; in front the garden drops away toward his favourite valley; while to the right he can look down into the upper part of the same valley and over the tops of trees to the rising land that leads up toward the hill country of South Wales. If on a fine summer's morning, when all Nature is smiling on the works of his hands, he is tempted to feel some pride in what he has accomplished, there will be few to declare that the feeling is not justified.

93 Garden facade from the shrub bank

In practice, there was never to be another summer when Tipping's sense of achievement at Mounton was not overshadowed by anxiety. His own July 1917 article on the gardens, for all its description of their beauty – 'promisingly gay by May' of 1914 and 'fully clothed' with vines and rambling roses by 1916 when the photographs were taken – concludes with a gloomy quotation from Oliver Goldsmith's poem 'The Deserted Village', a reflection on 'vain transitory splendours'. Noting how 'the outbreak of war revolutionised conditions' just at the moment when the work of creation was complete, he writes:

> Since then there has been no thought of extensions and developments, but a somewhat wearying effort to carry on while the effective staff is dispersed over sea and land . . . To prevent buildings from becoming ruinous and gardens reverting to wilderness is now the utmost realisable aim. Far behind us seem the easy affluent times when everyone was making, enlarging, perfecting and adorning gardens. How many of these little paradises of recent creation are doomed to future waste? Will merely *a few torn shrubs* mark the spot
> *Where once the garden smil'd*
> *And still where many a garden flower grows wild?*

94 David Lloyd George, who visited Mounton with his family for lunch and to see the gardens in 1914
95 Women Land Workers in 1917. Tipping wrote several articles in *Country Life* about the training of women as farm and garden workers in wartime

The essential problem was a lack of manpower. From January 1916 single men aged 18 to 41 were liable to be called up for military service. From May 1916 conscription was extended to married men, and eventually the age limit was increased to 51. Tipping had calculated that Mounton required ten full-time gardeners but soon both horticultural apprentices and experienced men had gone. Noting that the pink roses he had chosen for the pergola area were subject to mildew and needed expert attention, he wrote, 'With gardeners battling against the German pest it is difficult to deal adequately with these home enemies.' By the end of the war the borders must have been overgrown and the lawns unkempt, and it was from around this time that the local people began to speak of Mounton as 'Tipping's folly'. Entertainment was also out of the question as news came in of the deaths of local men and the sons of friends. Eric Francis, the architect of the house and Tipping's protégé, had joined up, leaving work at Wyndcliffe Court unfinished. Lady Celia Congreve, one of his oldest friends, served as a nurse in Belgium and France although she was in her late forties, while her son Billy was killed in action in 1916, winning a VC.

Tipping, who turned 60 in 1915, played his part as well as he could. He let Mathern Palace, which was now empty, for 25 Belgian refugees and provided material for the women of Mathern and Mounton to makes shirts for the Chepstow Company of Territorials. Edward Hudson had immediately pledged the resources of *Country Life* to the war effort (fig.96). The issue of 15 August 1914 called on the upper classes 'to live sparingly' and articles followed on increasing food supply from farms and domestic gardens, on collecting fruits and berries from hedgerows, and on giving up horses treasured as hunters for use at the front. Tipping's articles on country houses and gardens continued but other articles reflected war concerns. In June 1915 he wrote about the use of village institutes to feed children in rural areas, as was already happening at Eglwysbach, where 61 children received a two-course meal of 'bone-forming ingredients' daily under the direction of Lady Conway of Bodnant Hall. Closer to his own interests, he encouraged the training of women as farm and garden workers, describing how Miss Thorne, a woman gardener he had recruited for Mounton, had developed a programme for 40 local wives and daughters who were able to work part-time (fig.95). Their first task, 'weeding a ten-acre field of autumn-sown wheat which was moderately foul with thistles and docks', was also designed to weed out any volunteers who were physically incapable, but eventually a good number were employed as garden assistants, releasing older men and boys to help with hay-making and harvest. Tipping noted that

pay was only 3d. an hour, a third of what a skilled woman could earn in a factory, but they were able to stay at home and the work was done not 'from personal necessity, but rather as a patriotic duty' which also brought together 'for a useful and national purpose women of various classes and aptitudes'.

Tipping did not immediately lose faith that Mounton could again become the show house it was intended to be. In 1917 he bought 1640 acres of the Trellech estate, 11 miles away, selling off some of the land, cottages and farmhouses almost immediately but keeping a considerable area for rough shooting as an added attraction for visiting friends. However, the human and economic costs of the war meant that the carefree days of the Edwardian period were a thing of the past. Nearly a million British servicemen had been killed and almost 2 million had been permanently disabled. British economic output fell by 25 per cent between 1918 and 1921, the country lost its place as the great exporter to the world as industry in the United States grew stronger, and it has been argued that the peace heralded a 20-year great depression. There was a disproportionately high percentage of casualties among the landed classes and although Tipping had lost no immediate relatives – there were none – many of his friends had, and grand parties now seemed inappropriate. It is significant that my biography of Tipping's life is titled *Edwardian Country Life* (2011). He lived until he was 78 but the years 1901–14 were the time of his flourishing, and Mounton was to be his crowning achievement. Sadly the mood of the brief summer of 1914 could not be recaptured when the war came to an end.

96 Wartime in *Country Life*: Chequers was used as a voluntary hospital for wounded soldiers, 1914–16; Tipping let Mathern Palace for Belgian refugees
97 (overleaf) Original Brasted Urn with new topiary on bowling green

98 Book shelf end with family crest from Mounton House belonging to Tipping and given to the Holden family

6. DECLINE AND FALL

Mounton House and gardens, created extravagantly from nothing and designed as an object lesson and joy to be shared, became a liability and reproach during and after the First World War, and within four years of the war's end Tipping turned his back on them. He was fortunate that he did not have to sell everything and see his losses in stark economic terms; rather, he was wealthy enough simply to give it away.

Tipping then built his third Monmouthshire home, High Glanau (fig.99), 12 miles away and occupying part of the land he had bought near Trellech. Although it, too, was built (in 1922–3) with the collaboration of Eric Francis, is in the Arts and Crafts style, and has both formal and wild gardens (1922–9), it provides a marked contrast to Mounton. Both houses have magnificent views, but Mounton looks south, towards England and beyond the estuary to the Atlantic, while High Glanau looks west, inland to the Welsh mountains, as if Tipping was retreating from the wider world. The nearest town was Monmouth, a market town deep in a valley, whereas Mounton had been close to Chepstow, a busy port. The new house had only one major reception room (fig.100) and two small guest bedrooms. Tipping described it as 'a cottage', and instead of exemplifying the best of four distinct periods as at Mounton the interior was more harmonious, thoroughly masculine and sober, favouring plasterwork ceilings, oak panelling, and furniture and decoration of the Elizabethan and Jacobean eras (fig.101). Tipping continued as architectural editor of *Country Life* until 1930, as well as contributing gardening articles to the *Observer* and *Morning Post*; he designed gardens at Wyndcliffe Court near Chepstow (1922) and Dartington Hall, Devon (1928); but he had lost the sight of one eye by the war's end and the years before his death in 1933, aged 78, were no longer marked by social ambitions. In 1925 he sold his hospitable London home in Dorset Square, exchanging it for the suburban setting of Harefield House (fig.102) in north-west Middlesex. It was an easy commute to central London when he needed to consult libraries or attend editorial meetings; he took part in village life in a small way and designed another remarkable garden (fig.103) for himself; but it was quieter, another sign of withdrawal.

Meanwhile Mounton was passed into the hands of worthy new owners. Before his death in 1911 William Fearon Tipping (fig.104), knowing that Henry Avray would inherit the entire family wealth as the sole survivor, asked if on his own death he would make some kind of bequest to William's godson Hubert Holden (fig.106). Tipping fulfilled that request early and generously when the Mounton House estate was transferred to Holden on his discharge from the Royal Artillery in 1922. Hubert Capel Lofft Holden was then 33, had held a commission for 12 years and achieved the rank of major. His grandfather, from an old Staffordshire family, was a distinguished classical scholar; his father was Brigadier-General Sir Henry Capel Lofft Holden KCB FRS, and he could trace descent through the female line to Arthur Capel, who in 1661 was created Viscount Malden and Earl of Essex (after the extinction of the earlier title). Hubert came to Mounton with his wife of five years, Margaret, and their three young children; a fourth was born soon afterwards (fig.107). Tipping had given them a considerable sum of money to help with expenses but it was still a huge responsibility to take on a large estate with a 20,000 square foot house, fully furnished with valuable pieces, and numerous outbuildings. The staff consisted of four gardeners and a groom outside, a cook, pantry maid, butler, footman and two housemaids inside, with the addition of a nanny and nursemaid while the children were young, and later a governess. Heating the house and employee cottages required 300 tons of coal a year. Nevertheless, they maintained the house and gardens well (fig.108) until 1936, helped no doubt by the availability of male labour in the years of the Depression (Tipping was a great employer of local men for laying out paths through the woods at High Glanau).

When the Holdens moved to Ashton Manor in Devon they sold Mounton to neighbours, the Liddell family, for £5,000 – a quarter of what the house alone had cost to build. Charles Liddell was one of the founding Partners of Liddell Bros, shipping merchants at Shanghai and Hankow (now Wuhan). He had returned from China in 1900 and moved into Shirenewton Hall (fig.109) near Chepstow, where he created a notable Japanese garden. In 1928 his son Percy William Oswald Liddell, who had taken over direction of the firm, also came back to Britain with his wife and five children, no doubt because the political instability of China made trade impossible. The family stayed with Percy's father at Shirenewton for several years and then was delighted when Mounton House, just three miles away, became available; they certainly had the means to maintain it. They were there for 12 years, six of them during the Second World War, and they were lucky that the house was not requisitioned as a school or rehabilitation home for the wounded, or (with its southern exposure) as a tuberculosis sanitarium.

Even so, Mounton played its part in the war effort. Gwendoline Liddell was appointed as the county organiser for the Women's Voluntary Service and administered the local billeting of children evacuated from the cities. As many as five thousand local women were recruited to serve in various roles and Mounton's long gallery, with its independent entrance from the courtyard, must have provided an ideal headquarters. Also, sections of the grounds were ploughed up and used for food production in the Dig for Victory campaign.

99 High Glanau near Monmouth, Tipping's retirement cottage built in 1923

100 (overleaf) Central sitting room at High Glanau
101 (pp 100–01) Tipping's study where he wrote his books and articles for *Country Life*

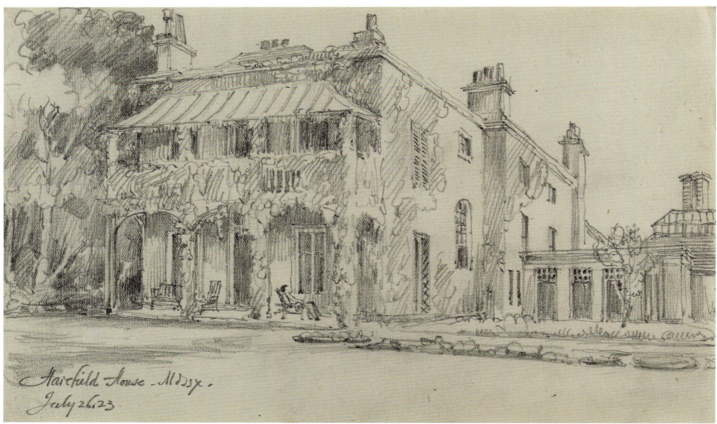

102 Harefield House in Middlesex, which Tipping bought in 1925. Pencil sketch by G.H. Kitchin
103 Tipping sitting in the garden at Harefield House. He died there of cancer in 1933. Pencil sketch by G.H. Kitchin

104 Tipping's brother William Fearon Tipping, godfather to Hubert Holden
105 Bess Holden, adored by William Fearon Tipping, with her son Hubert Holden who inherited Mounton House
106 The wedding of Hubert Holden and Margot Knight-Bruce, 20 January 1917, five years before they inherited Mounton House
107 The Holden family photographed at Mounton House in 1926

108

The Liddells lost their son Ian (fig.110) to a sniper's bullet just a month before VE Day and the other children were grown up, so the house was put on the market in 1948. The advertisement from Hampton & Sons mentions that Mounton was 'the subject of an illustrated article in *Country Life*' and had been 'built by Mr. H. Avray Tipping for his own occupation'. It lists 'five fine reception rooms' (counting Tipping's work room and library), 'twelve principal bed and dressing rooms', six bathrooms, six staff bedrooms and a 'nursery suite' (which was certainly not part of Tipping's original design!); the gallery is described as a 'magnificent ballroom 84 ft long'; beyond the house there were 'garages, stabling and four superior cottages, lovely gardens and grounds extending in all to about 22 acres'. In spite of all these attractions the agents were not optimistic about a sale, at least to private owners. In the post-war world those who had worked in domestic service now sought better-paid jobs in the cities, and the Labour government increased inheritance taxes just when estate incomes had fallen off. It was difficult for a family to keep a country house running and this is the age when many fine houses were demolished. The advertisement concluded that Mounton House was 'eminently suitable for hotel, school, etc.'; that was the best that could be hoped for and that is what happened.

The house was originally purchased in 1948 to be a school for deaf children, with plans to carry out the necessary modifications drawn up by Sir Percy Thomas (1883–1969), but after various bureaucratic delays it was eventually sold on to the Monmouthshire Education Committee to become the 'Residential Special School for Delicate Children' which the county felt it needed. Fortunately Tipping was dead by then, because he would have been distressed to see the undoing of his integrated vision for the land: cottages were sold off, areas – including the rose garden – were ploughed up for agricultural use, and another 11 acres were left for hay. The house needed to be re-roofed and there was pressure from the Ministry of Education in London to use the cheapest slate available; fortunately the local committee was able to appeal for extra money so

108 The tea house used as a croquet pavilion in the Holdens' time. They still opened the gardens for fetes and in aid of charities until they left in 1936

109 Shirenewton Hall near Chepstow, the home of the Liddell family
110 Captain Ian Oswald Liddell VC, photographed in the great parlour at Mounton

111 1948 *Country Life* sale notice for Mounton House

that Westmorland slate could be used. Work was complete by August 1953 and the school opened in September, catering to up to 80 children and designed to allow them to continue their education while they returned to full health (fig.112).

A Ministry of Education inspection and report in 1956 reveals not only that the school was doing a good job but also that much of the interior had been preserved:

> Few special schools are accommodated in premises of such distinction as this. The main building of two storeys in grey stone with slate roofs, in fifteen acres of parkland and natural gardens, was in excellent condition when purchased and has been very well maintained. The original drawing room, dining room, library and ancillary rooms have panelled walls and decorative plaster ceilings, while the bedrooms provide most attractive dormitories for the girls and command wide views of a wooded and undulating countryside. Three classrooms were contrived from the former ballroom and annexe.

Through the years of the baby boom the school was full and much appreciated, but in the 1960s, with improved social conditions, there were fewer 'delicate' children in the sense of poor physical health, and a 1969 survey suggested that the school should focus on 'deprived and emotionally disturbed children', although objecting that the main house was 'too dreary, inconvenient and old fashioned'. Even so, Mounton House continued as a special residential school for another 30 years, until new premises were built and the main estate was put up for sale. It was then that Cadw, the Welsh government's historic environment service, took an interest, and in 2000 Mounton was listed for protection: 'included at II* as an important early C20 country house, designed as a whole and constructed 1910–1912 by H. Avray Tipping and Eric Francis; and as a part of the significant layout consisting of the house, the ancillary buildings and the garden features which make a very complete landscape ensemble for the period'. Several of the estate buildings and garden areas such as the pergola and tea house were separately listed, but there were grave questions about the survival of this 'significant layout'.

112 (overleaf) Aerial view of Mounton House in 1960 when it was a school, showing the original Messenger & Co. glasshouses and kitchen garden and a prefab classroom in the west garden

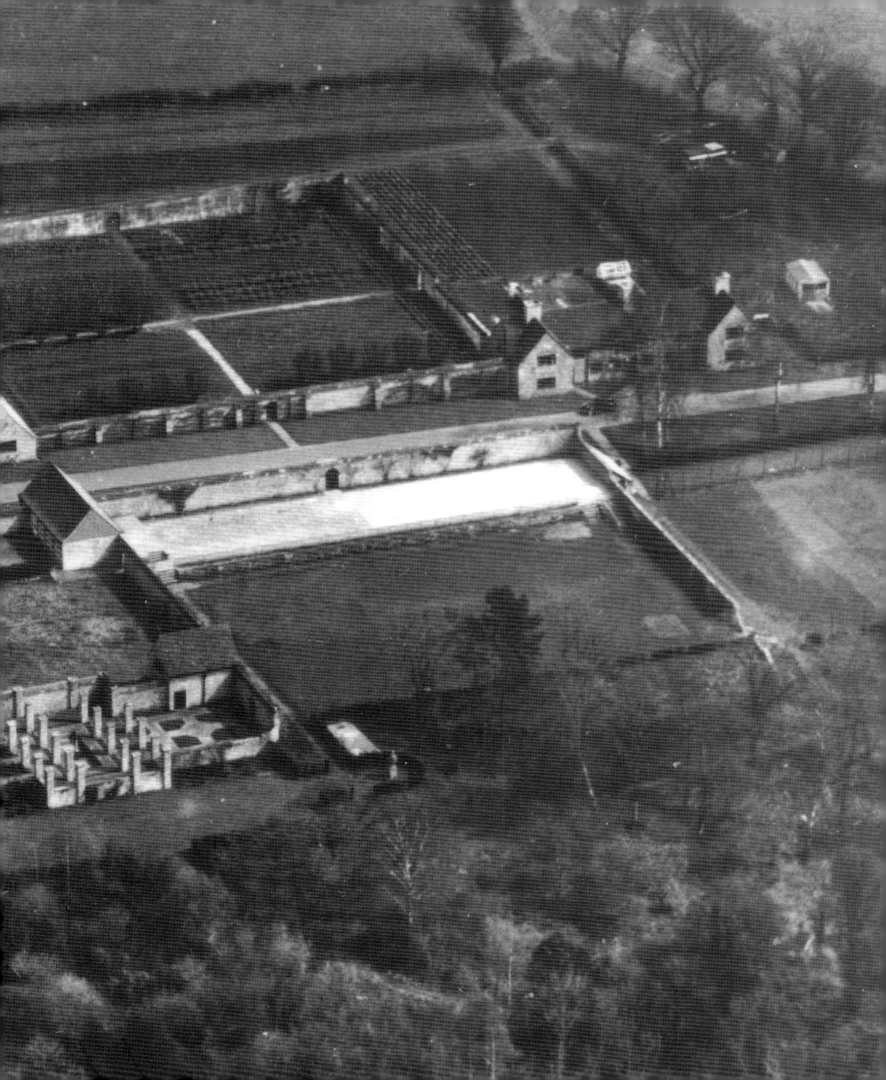

7. THE RECREATION OF A HOUSE

Gwent County Council sold the freehold of Mounton House and a substantial part of the land to Decourcy Finance in April 2002 and subsequently Crownwall Developments took over (fig.115). By that time most of the original garden layout was difficult to identify; now the interior, which had largely been left intact by the school, would also be obscured. With the new century and new-found prosperity country houses were being divided into apartments and timeshare accommodation. People noticed, as Tipping had a hundred years earlier, the juxtaposition of romanticism and convenience in the Chepstow area: its charming hills and views were close to the M48 and M4 motorways, making it commutable to Bristol and even to London. So, as Mounton House Park, the house and associated buildings were converted into 17 separate dwellings (fig.115). The developers did their work with plasterboard, fibreglass doors and laminate, and Tipping's vision seemed to be lost for ever.

The marketing prospectus for Mounton House Park mentions that it is 'situated in an area of outstanding natural beauty' yet 'approximately 18 miles from Bristol and within two miles of Chepstow'. It is clear about the Grade II* listed status of much of the property and that the refurbishment would be 'in accordance with building regulation approval, listed building consent and planning permission'. Residents would have 'the benefit of the communal grounds that incorporate the tennis court', although there was no promise to restore even a part of Tipping's garden; rather, most units had their own small private gardens. Of the 17 units, half were associated with the main house and half were reworkings of gardeners' cottages, laundry and stables (which had been converted to classrooms for the school). The plan shows that the main house was divided into four apartments (nos 1–4), the long gallery into two (5 and 6), and the kitchen areas into two more (7 and 8, with no.7 being new construction to the east of the forecourt where Tipping had had a service court and coal store). The original pricing for most of the units, released in late 2003 and early 2004, ranged from £140,000 to £250,000 according to size.

The present owners of Mounton House initially bought unit no.6, the north half of the gallery, with a view over the gorge to the west. They were working in Singapore and it provided a British bolthole, a complete contrast to life in that densely populated city, while not requiring any great maintenance or commitment. However, as they began to understand the history of the house and garden, they realised, as Tipping had in 1910, that much more could be done – and like him they were in a position to do it. In 2012 they

113 The finished great parlour with chandeliers and restored floors and woodwork

Project concept

Mounton House is a Grade 2* listed property, approximately 18 miles from Bristol and within 2 miles of Chepstow. Planning permission has been granted to allow its conversion to 17 residential units of various sizes situated within its own grounds, accessed via a substantial, well manicured private driveway with secure electric gates.

The properties will be refurbished in accordance with building regulation approval, listed building consent and planning permission. The nature of these works is detailed on the accompanying specification sheet. This allows prospective clients to purchase one of these properties at what we consider to be significantly below market prices — with the added benefit of being able to personalise the property to suit their own taste and requirements. The developer will also undertake all communal works, as defined in the specification.

Residents will have the benefit of the communal grounds that incorporate the tennis court and other impressive areas. The majority of units also have their own private gardens, garaging is available at an additional cost.

...situated in an area of outstanding natural beauty

bought units 3 and 4, two flats which occupied the east side of the main house. No.3 was a relatively small flat, spread over three floors with additional bedrooms in part of the attics – originally servants' rooms, which overlooked the forecourt and incorporated Tipping's work room with the Arts and Crafts fireplace which Eric Francis had designed. No.4 was the biggest flat, overlooking the garden and containing the great parlour, Tipping's library and its loggia, the ladies' sitting room and the entrance hall; upstairs was the area of Tipping's bedroom, and other fine barrel-ceilinged bedrooms.

In 2016 units 1 and 2 were purchased, adding the area of the dining room with its accompanying loggia and serving area, and the rest of the main house's bedrooms, so that they now had the whole living area of Tipping's Mounton, apart from the gallery; with unit 2 came the pergola garden. This meant the restoration of the main house could begin. They had already commissioned Earle Architects of London to remove modern additions and restore the original proportions and elegance of the structure in units 3 and 4. Now they asked Earle to prepare further designs for the reconfiguration of all four flats, involving all three levels of accommodation and an additional basement level which connected the entire length of the original building. Earle Architects are specialists in retrofitting, the process of modifying and modernising an existing building without spoiling it (they have had particular success in transforming a number of Art Deco cinemas). At Mounton the plans involved rediscovering and, where possible, restoring the historic rooms while still providing the amenities and comforts, and the efficiencies of operation, which 21st-century occupants expect.

This meant that the initial work was to remove all the insensitive modern partition walls, doors and stairs, together with the modern kitchen and bathroom fixtures and fittings that had been put in by the developers not much

Developers' project concept

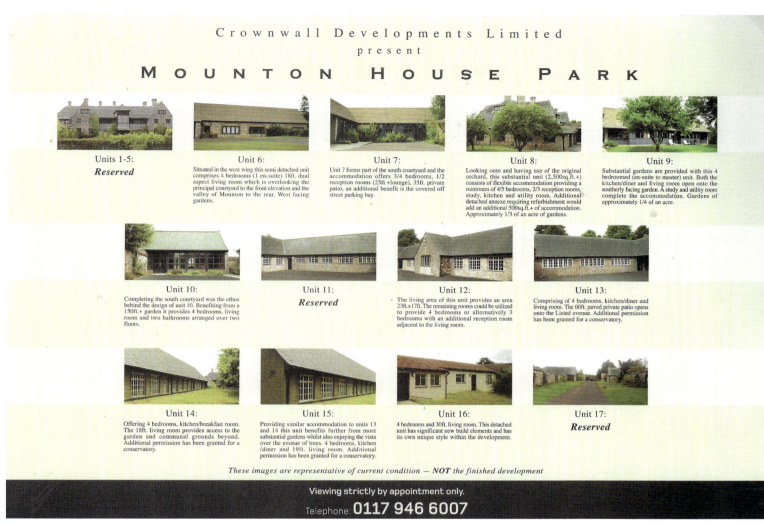

more than ten years before. The new owners' vision was to recreate the original integrity of the house, with all its Arts and Crafts features, not only outside but as far as possible inside.

One of the first tasks was to inspect the concrete slab from which the ornate plaster ceiling of the great parlour was suspended. It was supported by the masonry walls and two steel beams but some deterioration of the ferro-concrete was to be expected, especially as it was such an early example of the use of the material. Earle Architects asked Momentum Consulting Engineers to review the condition of the concrete slab and consider how new plumbing services could be routed under the concrete without damaging the moulded plaster ceiling of the room below, which largely survived. A pilot hole was made with a hand drill to establish the depth of the slab. This was found to be 100 mm (just under 4 inches), with a void beneath over the ceiling. Then a specialist core drill was used without water to make inspection holes, so that samples of the concrete could be taken without risk of them dropping into the void and through the ceiling (fig.116). It was found that there was sufficient room to run new service pipes between the top of the ceiling joists and the underside of the concrete and continuous welded pipework was used to minimise joints and the risk of leaks. This meant that the raised floor put in by the developers to conceal pipework could be removed. All areas were eventually re-plumbed and new en suite bathrooms for the master bedroom and dressing room were put in with fixtures of the highest quality.

In the great parlour itself countless layers of paint on the plaster ceiling meant that the fine details had been lost. A heavy-duty chemical paint remover was thickly applied with a spatula and then blanketed with a special laminated paper; this was left for 24 hours and then peeled back to reveal the decorative details. The same was done successfully with the much-repainted plasterwork of the dining room (fig.117).

115 Mounton House developed into 17 units

On the ground floor, carpet and any modern floor timbers were removed and the oak floors were reinstated (fig.118). In many places new skirting boards were made to match surviving pieces of the original design; likewise new oak panelling had to be made, and then stained and polished to the right shade to be unobtrusive (fig.120), and any half-timbering which had been obscured by partition walls was again exposed (fig.119).

The house was rewired and the modern lighting fixtures chosen by the developers were removed and replaced, with chandeliers finally returning to the parlour. All cables were chased into walls so that there was no ugly surface wiring. New cupboards were made to conceal fuse boxes and electrical meters and all sockets, internet and television points were carefully chosen in a bronze finish that would not stand out. Timber coving was made to hide special lighting designed to illuminate the plaster-ceilinged rooms.

For heating, all the existing radiators in the house were removed and replaced with new cast-iron traditional radiators (fig.121). Two large Worcester Bosch boilers were installed in the attic floor with a discharge flue through the roof void (fig.123). New oak radiator covers were made with brass woven wire panels for the great parlour, library

116 Core drilling the concrete slab without water, above the great parlour's plaster ceiling
117 Restoration of the plasterwork in the dining room

and master bedroom (fig.122), and trench heaters were also sunk into the floors of the parlour because it was such a large and high room to keep warm. All the chimneys were repaired, with new flue liners and fans added so that the open fires in the great parlour and Tipping's workroom were in working condition. Elsewhere a wood-burning stove and gas fires were employed.

Each room required some special attention. In the ladies' sitting room which had become the kitchen of unit 3, a new oak door was installed to access the terrace, and the original fireplace of 1720 was carefully restored (fig.124). In the library the oak shelving of 1913 was still present but had become rotten (fig.125); it was completely remade by a master carpenter (fig.127). In Tipping's workroom the ceiling was raised, exposing the top of Eric Francis's Arts and Crafts brick fireplace. This had been covered and the central brickwork of the fireplace had been removed; now new narrow bricks in the Italian style were made locally so that the fireplace could again become the dominant feature of the room (fig.126). A kitchen extension built by the developers to the north-east was demolished, opening up what had been a courtyard and allowing the reinstatement of the courtyard windows from the house.

118 Repair of the great parlour floor
119 Half-timbering that had been obscured by partitions exposed again, and the walls replastered
120 (overleaf) The great parlour door – repaired

121

122

123

121 Modern radiators were removed and traditional cast-iron radiators installed throughout the house
122 New oak radiator covers were made for the main rooms
123 Two Worcester Bosch boilers were installed in the attic to heat the whole house

124 The fireplace was restored in the ladies' sitting room
125 The library shelving was rotten and had to be removed
126 The Arts and Crafts fireplace in the workroom had been tampered with, so the ceiling height was restored and new bricks inserted

127 New bookcases and radiator covers in the library

The original dining room was restored (fig.128) and the marble floor, after carpeting had been removed, was acid cleaned (fig.129). However, there was a problem: an accompanying kitchen was needed but Tipping's extensive kitchen areas had become a separate residential unit. The problem was solved by the use of the loggia on the south-east of the house. This was much larger than the loggia on the other side and had been designed by Tipping for summer dining, with sliding doors to the south, opening onto the terrace and view. The sliding doors were remade as hinged and sealed doors which matched the originals exactly but more efficiently excluded any damp and cold brought by winter storms from the Atlantic (fig.130). Rather than contrive an Edwardian-style kitchen, which would have been impractical without a host of Edwardian servants, the architects recommended all the latest appliances. Nevertheless, within this thoroughly modern setting it was possible to preserve a plaque that had been set into the walls of the original loggia. This is a copy of a Latin inscription on the walls of the cathedral of Como, recalling how the building of a new, Gothic cathedral began in 1396 and honouring 'Thomas de Rodaris' (Tommaso Rodari, 1460–1525), who served as director of the lengthy project for nearly 25 years (fig.132). Another plaque in the open loggia (fig.131) is a terracotta rendering, probably from the 19th century, of Piero della Francesca's fresco (1451) of Sigismondo Pandolfo Malatesta (1417–1468) in San Francesco, Rimini. Tipping perhaps kept it as a private joke among his cultured friends because, although Sigismondo was a great military strategist and patron of the arts, he was also famously immoral (the historical novel about him by the aesthete Edward Hutton, published in 1906, had just brought him back to public knowledge).

The upstairs presented different problems. With flats on two or three levels, the developers had put in new staircases. These were removed and Tipping's staircase from the main hall again became the principal means of access, with matching new balusters made when necessary. The original staircase had been open; in the time of the school, probably to meet fire regulations, there was a wall, door and window at the top landing (fig.133). These were removed and replaced, in the interests of energy efficiency, with a more subtle transition between stairs and bedroom corridor. At the top of the staircase a frameless glass wall was made, protected by a wooden balustrade which matched the medieval style of the original stairs (fig.134). Beside it, a frameless double glass door was erected to open onto the restored upper corridor which once again ran the length of the whole house. The developers had severely narrowed Tipping's generous and well-proportioned corridor as a way to find extra space for bathrooms in the flats (fig.135).

128 The dining room was repainted and the marble floor acid cleaned

129 (overleaf) The completed dining room

131

130 (opposite) A new kitchen was made from the open dining loggia with new sealed and hinged doors
131 The plaque of Sigismondo Pandelfo Malatesta in the wall of the open loggia
132 (overleaf) The plaque on the wall of the new kitchen, a copy from Como Cathedral that Tipping bought in 1912

CVM HOC TEMPL[VM]
FECTVM ESSET A[...]
RENOVARI CEPTVM E[...]
HVIVS VERO POSTERI[...]
FVNDAMENTA MDX[...]
FRONTIS ET LATER [IA...]
THOMAS DE

133

Earle Architects were asked to demolish all these encroaching plasterboard walls, together with the cupboards and bathrooms they concealed, and the correct scale of the upper floor was revealed, filled now with natural light, both functional and beautiful (fig.137).

In Tipping's own bedroom, the central door had been moved and had to be reinstated; new panelling was installed on either side and matched to the original panelling (fig.138). The ceiling in Tipping's bedroom, with its moulded plaster, had been water damaged and had to be repaired and repainted (fig.139). In many of the bedrooms new panelling had to be made (figs 140 and 141) and fireplaces and hearths were restored (it was not too difficult to discover where they had been because of the position of the chimneys) (fig.142). The architects found dry rot on the attic floor which had housed servants so a new staircase was made (fig.143). The traditional leaded windows were removed for restoration.

134

133 The top of the main staircase had been glazed in the 1950s when the house was a school
134 A new light glass wall was installed, echoing the original damaged banisters
135 On the first floor the original corridor had been cut in half by the developers
136 Landings were opened up to reveal the correct scale
137 (overleaf) The completed corridor

138

140

139

141

138 The door and panelling had been moved in Tipping's bedroom, so had to be reinstated
139 The ceiling in Tipping's bedroom had been water damaged and had to be repaired and repainted
140 The architects removed a bathroom to reinstate the original barrel ceiling and central door
141 Door and panelling renewed in the summer bedroom

142

143

142 The fireplace in one of the bedrooms was completely restored
143 Dry rot was found on the attic floor so a new floor and staircase had to be made

Tipping's fondness for walls and paved areas in the immediate vicinity of the house meant that Earle Architects also had to advise on the restoration of these architectural features, although under the guidance of the garden designer, Arne Maynard, so that nobody should forget that they were primarily settings for plants. The original stone paving on the terrace had been stolen while the developers were working on the property, so a new terrace was laid with stones of random sizes to match what had been put down in 1912 (fig.144). Fortunately the photos in the *Country Life* archive, many more than those that had accompanied the contemporary articles on Mounton, were available as a guide. In the 1970s the school had put in a practical but ugly covered walkway at the west end of the house; this was demolished to expose the original west facade with its half-timbering and the door into the west garden was reinstated. The coped walls at either end of the terrace, designed to protect the sitting areas on the south side from Atlantic winds, both survived but their wooden doors had disappeared. The remains of them were found lying in the garden, rotted away from damp and almost unrecognisable (fig.145), but they provided enough of a pattern for a master carpenter to remake them in oak (fig.146).

The astonishing 24-pillar pergola required special treatment because it was listed for protection: two of the stone pillars were missing and Cadw insisted that they should be replaced in wood so that the authentic and the new could be distinguished (fig.147); new green oak rafters were made to match the originals (fig.148). The rectangular lily pool was completely restored and a new copy of the fountain in the form of a water-spouting boy was found (fig.149). The plumbing for the lily pool and fountain was decayed beyond repair so specialist water engineers were employed to devise a new system. The Bulbeck Foundry, which has provided leadwork for many distinguished buildings in the last 33 years, including royal residences, was commissioned to make water cisterns on either side of the pool. Water from these feeds the pool and fountain before flowing into a larger lead cistern on the wall beneath the pergola (fig.150). In association with this, a borehole was drilled to a depth of 200 ft, ensuring a constant supply of water at steady pressure to several different areas of the garden, including the rock garden pools (fig.151).

144 The terrace was in a derelict state so new random-sized stones were laid to match the original
145 Oak doors that sat within the coped walls were found rotten and lying in the garden
146 (opposite) New oak doors were made by a master carpenter

147 Two missing pillars were replaced in oak

148 New green oak rafters were made
149 (overleaf) A new fountain in the form of a water-spouting boy was found and erected in the lily pool
150 (pp. 140–1) Bulbeck Foundry lead cistern below the pergola

The open-sided two-storey tea house, also a listed building, required painstaking restoration. Tipping had a special fondness for it as a place to sit in the shade while watching croquet games and taking tea with friends, and also for summer sleeping on the upper deck, which was open to the night air. After nearly a century of neglect the developers had found it in a derelict condition and had not attempted any repairs. The new owners had new roof timbers installed and the oak facade completely remade to preserve it for their own use and for the future (figs 152–156).

As well as carpenters with the skills to handle large beams and woodwork of heritage quality, a team of stone masons was needed. They repaired the stone walls of the house and surrounding areas and repointed them when necessary (fig.157), but some of the garden walls required special sensitivity because they were built without mortar to host plants. In two articles in *The Garden* of 1917, titled 'Dry wall gardening at Mounton House', Tipping had stated: 'Dry wall building is a job for the gardener himself to undertake rather than the mason. The principle on which the latter is trained is to build walls perfectly perpendicular, completely weather-tight, hostile to plant life'; the mason is thus 'a real danger to the success of the dry wall as the home of alpines'. Tipping claimed that at Mounton 'the making of my own dry walls has been entirely gardener's work', with building and planting taking place at the same time – 'as each tier of stones was laid, the right plants could be laid in between and upon them'. Obviously the walls could not be completely

151 A bore hole was drilled to ensure a constant supply of water for the gardens
152 (opposite) A crane lifting the new facade into place
153 (overleaf) Restoration of the tea house, with new roof timbers and a completely new oak facade

154 All hands needed to place the new facade into the correct position
155 An exact fit!
156 (opposite) The restored tea house

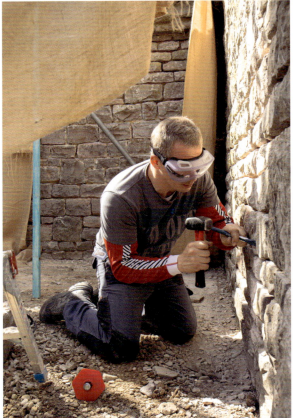

157

158

159

157 The exterior walls had to be repointed with lime render, and protected from frost with sacking
158 Example of stonework made up by Arne Maynard Garden Design
159 A stonemason laying paths with stone edging
160 (opposite) The new Diana statue was winched into place before the octagonal pool was made around it

rebuilt using this method but the masons had to distinguish between those walls that need to be well sealed and those where chinks must be left for future plantings. Other specialist craftsmen repaired some of the many paths and laid new ones (fig.158–9). Stone paths and flags had often been frost damaged, while the natural paths leading down to the gorge had almost disappeared in the course of more than a century.

The various garden ornaments which Tipping had placed so carefully to complement the layout of the gardens were largely missing or damaged. A new copy of the statue of Diana for the bowling green below the pergola was made in Italy but found in Amsterdam, and shipped to South Wales for placement on an Italian plinth, made to match the original, within its octagonal pool (fig.160). As before, it was surrounded by a circle of clipped yew and matched the axis of the pergola. On the other axis (parallel to the terrace, more east to west) and emphasising the length of the bowling green were the Brasted urns which Tipping had brought from his family home in Kent. They had survived but required minute repair by a stone mason from Hereford Cathedral. There was also new statuary. To delineate the transition from formal lawns to the slopes towards the gorge, the owners placed Magdalena Abakanowicz's (1930–2017) powerful bronzes *The Group of Five* (2014), with simple stone flags set into the lawn to lead to it (fig.161). At one of the viewpoints looking towards the estuary and the Somerset hills beyond there is Ugo Rondinone's (b.1964) *The Sun at 12 a.m.* (2019), a 306 cm (10 ft) circle of branches cast in bronze and gilded, which draws attention to the place while inviting the viewer to look beyond (fig.162).

As in the house, the restoration also enabled improvements beyond all Edwardian imagination: in the entrance drive two EV charging stations, mounted on oak posts, were concealed in one of the flowerbeds. Thanks to architects who understood the vision of the owners and the hard work of a host of craftsmen, Mounton House and its associated architectural features were returned to a state that Tipping would have recognised (figs 164–5). And yet the passage of a hundred years had made a difference: the house was far more efficient and environmentally friendly, it could be run without a dozen indoor staff, and it had become much more of a home.

161 (opposite) Magdalena Abakanowicz, *The Group of Five*, 2014
162 Ugo Rondinone, *The Sun at 12 a.m.*, 2019
163 (overleaf) *Group of Five* above the steep woodland path and view to the Severn Estuary

164 The oak stud panelling on the front of the house had been painted black and white by the developers

165 The front facade stripped back to original oak
166 (overleaf) Entrance courtyard with new topiary and pleached hedging
167 (pp 158–9) Summer planting on the terrace with topiary and copper and stone pots

8. THE RESURRECTION OF A GARDEN

Within Mounton House, the main work involved stripping away the accretions of modern developers so that the original proportions could again be seen. Outside, the stonework required extensive repair. However, that was only the beginning of the work because the gardens were more than a casual setting for the house. The south-facing windows of the major rooms and the openings from the protected terraces were an encouragement to look out and discover the surrounding plantings, which were just as important to Tipping as the striking interiors. As Tim Richardson has written in *English Gardens in the Twentieth Century* (2005), Tipping 'displayed a confident handling of formal features such as terraces and enclosed rose gardens, allowing them to segue together with more informal elements of the garden' and so offering guests an invitation to go beyond, to explore the grounds with their seasonal variety of colours and forms, and finally to see the view over the Severn Estuary. The gardens had suffered a century of neglect: almost as soon as they were complete in 1914 they lost the staff needed to maintain them, and in the last fifty years they had been abandoned. The rough outlines of Tipping's plan might still be distinguished but the carefully chosen and situated plants, the *raison d'être* for everything, were no more.

To this wilderness the owners were able to bring an outstanding garden designer, Arne Maynard, who was able not merely to restore but rather to transform and greatly enhance each of the different areas of the garden. Arne developed an interest in gardens as a teenager in Dorset. After an initial training in architecture, which he abandoned as a career but which proved useful later for projects like Mounton, he worked in a nursery in West London, creating small courtyard gardens. Some of his London customers, unwittingly seduced by the country-living dream which Tipping had propagated, also had weekend homes in the country, so Arne found himself advising on much larger spaces. In 2000, with Piet Oudolf, he designed (and grew the plants for) the *Gardens Illustrated* garden at the Royal Horticultural Society's Chelsea Flower Show, and they were the first newcomers to win Best in Show. Fully aware of the slavery to fashion at Chelsea, he nevertheless returned in 2012 with the Laurent Perrier Bicentenary Garden – what he called 'a real gardener's garden' rather than just a beautiful structure – and was awarded another Gold Medal. With the foundation of Arne Maynard Garden Design and the formation of a team, he has been able to create and restore important gardens in Britain and around the world, including a palace garden for the Queen of Jordan.

168 (opposite) The Diana statue seen from the water garden

169 Arne Maynard's proposal for the south garden

Thus Arne brought to Mounton nearly 25 years of varied experience, and there was a further happy coincidence. From the 1990s he had lived at Guanock House, a historic monastic building where the garden had to be created from nothing over the course of ten years in an uncultivated Lincolnshire field of 5 acres. It was near Spalding, the centre of British bulb growing, and the flatness of the fens meant that the garden was largely made up of secluded and protected areas, rather like the immediate surroundings of the house at Mounton. However, as a largely formal garden, it demanded the constant attention of a hands-on gardener, which Arne was eventually unable to give it. In 2006 he bought Allt y bela, a late medieval tower house set in a steep South Wales valley where the landscape presented new challenges, no longer permitting a symmetrical layout (fig.169). So when he came to Mounton ten years later he also had an understanding of wilder areas and the need to create smooth transitions from formal to natural. Moreover, Allt y bela is near Usk and just 12 miles from Mounton, so that Arne was able to supervise the work closely. He was very much the right man in the right place at the right time.

Arne first visited Mounton in September 2016 and shortly afterwards submitted design ideas to the owners (figs 169 and 171). That meant he was there for the whole period of the restoration of the architectural features, making sure that they were at the service of the garden as Tipping would have wanted. He noted the calm and elegant atmosphere of the house interior, with its regard for craftsmanship and quality of materials, and wrote, 'These are the characteristics that we would like to bring to or enhance throughout the garden.' He had access to the 1915 and 1917 *Country Life* articles on the house and gardens and their accompanying photos, as well as to the series of 12 more technical articles on aspects of the Mounton gardens

produced for *The Garden* between 1910 and 1921. It did not take long for Arne to realise that he and Tipping were kindred spirits in many ways. Both designed gardens for others but were passionate about their own gardens. Both were writers, with Arne regularly contributing to *Gardens Illustrated*. They were practical gardeners, aware of differing seasons, soils and climatic settings, even if Tipping had someone else to do the spade work; and both were real plantsmen, willing to experiment and learn, with a vast knowledge of and love for different varieties.

Arne's time in South Wales had moved his thinking on the balance between natural and formal. Here he is in 2020: 'I'm manipulating nature, taming it slightly. I like to place plants in areas that replicate their natural habitat, but it's very much a case of trial and error to see what works.' Here is Tipping, writing 120 years earlier, yet in very similar terms: 'The best of gardening is perhaps to lovingly tend one of Nature's choice spots, to remove what injures, and to heighten what improves its form, to vary and stimulate its flora, to retain the grace and feeling of the wild, while adding the eclectic richness and reasoned beauty of the cultured.'

However, Arne wanted to do much more than simply reproduce Tipping's Mounton. In the course of a century horticulture had changed dramatically, with new powered tools and techniques, new plants and hardier varieties which could now survive at the edge of the plateau – and, of course, Arne brought to Mounton his own unique experiences, knowledge and gifts. Thus his proposal to the owners clearly states: 'We'd like to bring the historical garden back to its former glory, in a sensitive interpretation of Avray Tipping's original vision, but at the same time create a garden of today which reflects your own taste and particular garden passions.'

---

170 Arne Maynard's own home, Allt y bela in Monmouthshire

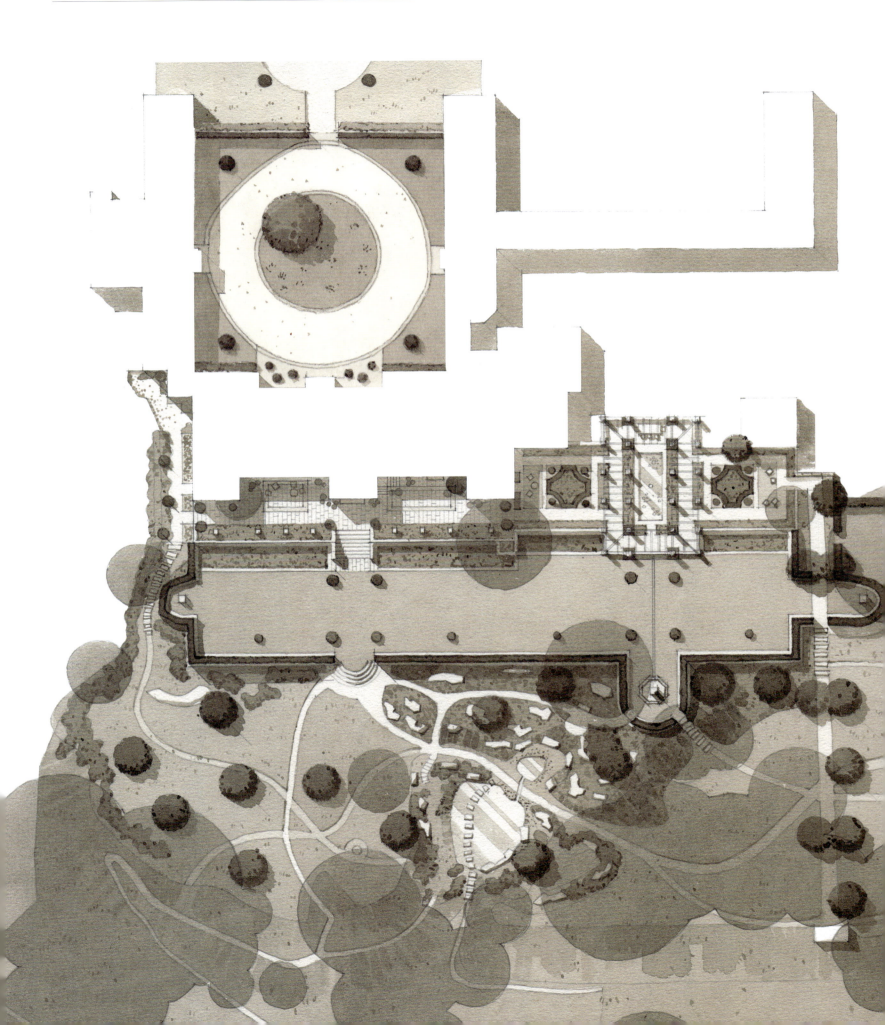

As with the house, each area required special treatment. Arne appreciated the shelter and seclusion of the terrace and the calm 'green' view towards the woodland, but he widened the original border above the retaining wall (fig.171) to allow for a much greater volume of planting which would soften the architecture and recreate an Edwardian feeling. One of Arne's gifts is a sense of colour, and his team put together mood boards of plants to discuss with the owners. The purpose, as the 2016 proposal stated, is

> to create borders which change over the seasons from the excitement of the spring bulbs, to the main show of mid-summer roses and iris, mixed with geraniums, nepetas, digitalis, and salvias, with a wonderful last peak of flowers for late summer, with plants such as the asters and dahlias, Japanese anemones, sanguisorbas and persicarias, many of which will hold on to seed heads over the winter.

At the west end a magnificent magnolia was pruned but preserved, its colours completely in harmony with the newer garden. The design team also advised on more tender plants, set in substantial pots of copper and stone, and on furniture for the terrace (fig.172).

Below the terrace wall he placed a deep herbaceous border whose plants reach up and almost mingle with the ones above, so that together they have 'the strength to sit in front of the bold architecture of the house'. The borders are filled with tulips and white hyacinth in spring (fig.173), followed by a romantic mix of delphiniums, irises and perennials like *Achillea ptarmica*, monarda and astrantia through the summer (fig.174), and finally Michaelmas daisies and dahlias for autumn colour (fig.175). The borders also soften Tipping's rather stark bowling green, the formal lawn framed by dark yews, and Arne has further improved the area by adding additional topiary, as in so many areas of the garden. The owners visited Solitair Nursery in Belgium to select four massive topiary yews clipped like wedding cakes to make an impact as one descends the steps from the terrace, each one slightly different to give interest even when the herbaceous borders have finished flowering. Arne also used copper beech topiary to punctuate the long lawn and tie in with the magnificent mature copper beech probably planted when the garden was laid out in 1912 (fig.176).

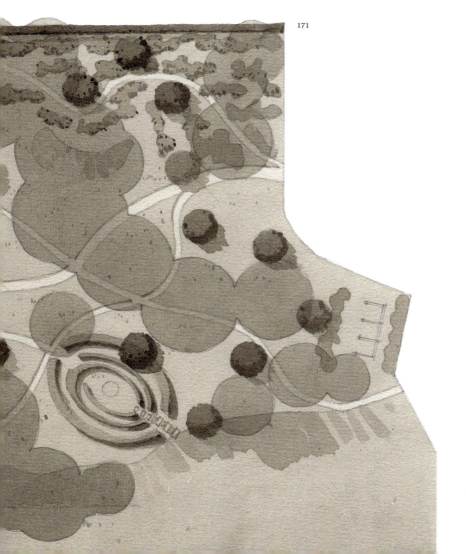

171

171 Developed Design Proposal, showing proposed planting of trees, topiary, herbaceous borders, hedging, shrubs, bulbs and rock garden
172 (overleaf) Arne widened the terrace borders – tulips and hyacinths in spring
173 (pp 168–9) New border on the bowling green lawn in early summer

174

He has an exceptional knowledge of the great variety of trees which can be clipped, pleached, pollarded and trained to add different shades and textures to a garden. Tipping, stuck with the traditional *Buxus* and *Taxus*, would have been delighted and amazed to see what is now possible.

To the east of the bowling green was an area which was unsatisfactory even in Tipping's time, described on his plan as 'shrub bank' and 'tree planted rough ground'. However, at its southern end, furthest from the house, there was a natural view point over the Severn Estuary (fig.178). Arne decided to make something of this, clearing the ground and planting an avenue of magnolias to lead to it (fig.177); the owners further enhanced the place with Ugo Rondinone's art installation. What had been an awkward no man's land became a destination.

The pergola garden was a blank slate. After advising on the renewal and extension of the whole water system and recommending new oak beams, Arne chose to make the formal pool 'the calm breathing space' at the centre and then surround it with a full immersion in flowers: 'dripping with roses hanging down from above, and from gaps between the stones of the terrace, full of the fabulous, swaying wands of *Dierama*' – the wandflower that Tipping had successfully pioneered at Mounton – 'and delicate *Dahlia merckii* whose flowers float on wiry stems . . . all punctuated with the spires of verbascums'. The formal garden enclosures on either side of the pergola were planted with hyacinths and tulips (fig.179), followed by roses and valerian in summertime (fig.180), and

175

174 Herbaceous border – the first summer after planting
175 Autumn planting

some winter flowering shrubs like daphnes; again topiary, in copper hues, was used to good effect (fig.181).

Beyond the bowling green, and to the south and west of the rock garden, many trees had self-seeded, obscuring the view and overshadowing more appropriate trees. Here Arne did some serious editing, creating space for Japanese flowering cherry trees in pink and white (fig.184) and then under-planting them with large numbers of bulbs and *Cyclamen coum* for the spring and *Cyclamen hederifolium* for the autumn; in this way the colour palette contributes to the unity of the whole layout. He also thinned the edge of the natural woodland which led down towards the gorge, making a more subtle transition by adding the double-flowered form of the native white cherry, *Prunus avium plena*, and planting woodland peonies in pink and white to bring together the wild and the cultivated. Most designers would have abandoned the steep woodland beyond, with its overgrown paths, but Arne saw what Tipping had seen, its 'magical and atmospheric' potential (fig.163). Although it was buried in leaf litter and brambles, he found that much of the original structure was in good order, with 'an amazing network of meandering paths, and steps cut into the banks held up by low walls'. The area was well worth recovering and enriching.

176 Tying in the original copper beech with clipped topiary on the bowling green lawn
177 An avenue of pink and white magnolias was planted
178 (overleaf) Opening of the view to the River Severn
179 (pp 174–5) The pergola garden with copper beech topiary and white hyacinths in spring

180 The pergola garden in summer
181 The formal garden enclosures either side of the pergola with topiary roses and valerian

182 The garden transformed – the west doorway and herbaceous border in September
183 Border looking east
184 (overleaf) Planting of Japanese cherries adjacent to the rock garden

Similarly, the rock garden was overgrown but deserved careful restoration and improvement because it was such an integral part of Tipping's plan, utilising the quarried ground there and providing a setting for the alpines that were a kind of obsession with his contemporaries. Arne excavated (fig.185) and repaired the original pools (fig.186), linking them with waterfalls to provide sound and movement (fig.187) and adding a shallow gravelled area for aquatic plants. He introduced new puddingstone rocks and more moss, and specimen trees and different varieties of Japanese maples were set in place before the numerous rock plants arrived – an operation that required many hands (fig.191). Nevertheless, he chose to plant the rock garden 'more simply than it would have been in Tipping's time, with plants that look naturally at home'. Again with an awareness of transitions and the power of colour to unite, the area adjacent to the rock garden has been planted with different varieties of wild cherry.

185 Placing of 250 puddingstone rocks to form the water gardens
186 Rocks in place and pools excavated
187 (opposite) Creating the pools and waterfalls
188 (overleaf) Brasted Urn on the bowling green, early morning
189 (pp 184–5) Planting of the rock garden with Arne Maynard's team and gardeners
190 (pp 186–7) Rock garden fully planted
191 (pp 188–9) The Rock Garden in Spring

192 Herbaceous border below the terrace looking east
193 Display of summer pots on the terrace
194 (opposite) Terrace steps with urns planted with salvias
195 (overleaf) Repaired Brasted urn above the yew hedge

Five years after Arne's initial proposal Mounton has been transformed. The views have been opened up, each major area has been refashioned and enhanced, and a seemingly endless list of new plants and trees has been introduced, both to harmonise with each other in colour and form and to complement the Arts and Crafts style of the house and its surroundings. And yet there is still more to do. There are plans for what had been Tipping's croquet lawn and parterre beyond the tea house, for the creation of a frame yard with wooden glasshouse, potting shed and cart shed, for a cutting garden and orchard, and for a new drive and parking area so that the forecourt can be rethought with bolder plantings, which will give a more dramatic entrance to the house. In a sense, the garden will never be finished, just as it was not complete in that distant summer of 1914 – and that should not be a cause of sadness. As Arne has wisely said, 'Gardens are about evolution and moving on, and you can't hold them still.' Mounton House and gardens have overcome the disappointments of Henry Avray Tipping who created them; they have survived and evolved; and as living organisms they will continue to convey beauty and peace.

196 (opposite) Diana statue sourced from Amsterdam and erected within an octagonal pool
197 The Diana statue seen from the pergola bay
198 (overleaf) Spring garden showing cherry trees
199 (pp. 198–9) Garden facade 2022

APPENDIX
Specialist suppliers, craftsmen and designers

Architect
Earle Architects
www.earlearchitects.com

Brick/tile restoration
Ned Heywood
www.blue-plaques.org.uk

Decorator
C.A. Price Painting and Decorating, Chepstow

Electrics
RCJ Electrical
www.rcjelectrical.com

Fireplace
Thornhill Galleries
www.thornhillgalleries.co.uk

Floor sockets
Cableduct Limited
www.cableductuk.com

Garden antiques
Architectural Heritage
www.architectural-heritage.co.uk
Piet Jonker
www.pietjonker.com

Garden design
AMGD
www.arnemaynard.com

Gardeners
Louis Moffett, Lucy Aiano, Leigh Watts

Glasswork and shower screens
Preedy Glass
www.preedyglass.com

Ironmongery
Comyn Ching
www.comynching.com

Joinery/carpentry
Miles Laughton Joinery
www.mileslaughtonjoinery.co.uk

Kitchen
Bulthaup
www.bulthaup.com

Landscaping
The London Garden Construction Company, London

Leaded windows
Brockweir Glass
www.brockweirglass.co.uk

Leadwork
Bulbeck Foundry
www.bulbeckfoundry.co.uk

Marble
Mandarin Stone
www.mandarinstone.com

Masonry
JB Masonry Ltd
www.jbmasonry.co.uk

Plumbing/heating
Plumbright
www.plumbrightheating.co.uk

Radiator grilles
James Gilbert and Son
www.jamesgilbertandson.com

Realistic gas fires
Neville Stephens and Allan Christensen, London

Reclaimed floorboards
Charlecotes Country House Interiors
www.originaloakflooring.com

Sanitary wares
C.P. Hart
www.cphart.co.uk

Topiary/trees
Solitair
www.solitair.be

Water features
Fairwater
www.fairwater.co.uk

BIBLIOGRAPHY

WORKS BY H. AVRAY TIPPING RELATED TO MOUNTON

Books

English Gardens, Country Life Ltd, London, 1925.
The Garden of To-day, Martin Hopkinson Ltd, London, 1933.

Articles

'Two renovated cottages in Monmouthshire', *Country Life*, 21 March 1908, pp 411–13.
'A water garden in the natural style', *Country Life*, 10 September 1910, pp 364–8.
'A water garden in the natural style', *The Garden*, 2 August 1913, pp 386–7.
'Some delightful spring shrubs I', *The Garden*, 3 June 1916, pp 272–3.
'Some delightful spring shrubs II', *The Garden*, 10 June 1916, pp 286–7.
'Tulips in the Mounton House garden', *The Garden*, 17 June 1916, pp 298–9.
'Dry wall gardening at Mounton House I', *The Garden*, 10 March 1917, pp 82–3.
'Dry wall gardening at Mounton House II', *The Garden*, 17 March 1917, pp 92–3.
'Rock gardening at Mounton House', *The Garden*, 14 April 1917, pp 122–3.
'Streamside gardening at Mounton House', *The Garden*, 28 April 1917, pp 142–3.
'The gardens of Mounton House, Chepstow', *Country Life*, 28 July 1917, pp 84–91.
'Mid-April in the Mounton House garden', *The Garden*, 24 April 1920, pp 206–7.
'Late April in the Mounton House garden', *The Garden*, 8 May 1920, pp 232–3.
'Sun lovers in the Mounton House gardens', *The Garden*, 2 July 1921, pp 326–7.
'Pears at Mounton House, Chepstow', *The Garden*, 24 September 1921, p.481.

OTHER SOURCES

Books

Aslet, Clive, *The Last Country Houses*, Yale University Press, London and New Haven, 1982.
Cornforth, John, *The Search for Style,* Andrew Deutsch, London, 1988.
Elliott, Brent, *The Country House Garden: From the Archives of Country Life,* Mitchell Beazley, London, 1995.
Festing, Sally, *Gertrude Jekyll,* Viking, London, 1991.
Gerrish, Helena, *Edwardian Country Life, The Story of H. Avray Tipping*, Frances Lincoln, London, 2011.
Hall, Michael, *The English Country House: From the archives of Country Life 1897-1939,* Michael Beazley, London, 1994.
Jekyll, Gertrude, *Wall and Water Gardens,* Country Life Ltd., London.
Jekyll, Gertrude, *Garden Ornament*, Country Life/Scribners, London and New York, 1918.
Maynard, Arne, *The Gardens of Arne Maynard*, Merrell Publishers, London, 2015.
Musson, Jeremy, *The English Manor House: From the Archives of Country Life,* Aurum Press, London, 1999.
Newman, John, *The Buildings of Wales: Gwent/Monmouthshire,* Penguin, London 2000.
Ottewill, David, *The Edwardian Garden*, Yale University Press, London, 1989.
Richardson, Tim, *English Gardens in the Twentieth Century: From the Archives of Country Life*, Aurum Press, London, 2005.
Tankard, Judith, *Gardens of the Arts & Crafts Movement,* Timber Press, Oregon, 2018.

Articles

Bowie-Sell, Daisy, 'Arne Maynard: "Gardens are about evolution and moving on, you can't hold them still"', *Gardens Illustrated*, 22 May 2020.
Conway, Martin, 'Mounton House, Chepstow, the residence of Mr. H. Avray Tipping', *Country Life*, 13 February 1915, pp 208–17.
Cornforth, John, 'Balancing Past and Present: The Country House between the Wars', *Country Life,* 8 January 1987, pp 80–4
Cox, E.H.M., 'A Passing Generation: Gardening Trends and Pioneers of the Last Thirty Years', *Country Life,* 24 June 1939, pp 667–9
Fitzherbert, S.W., 'Two Monmouthshire Gardens', *The Gardeners' Chronicle,* 6 October 1906 pp.240–2
Foster, Clare, 'The heavenly Monmouthshire garden of Arne Maynard', *House & Garden*, 6 May 2020.
Gerrish, Helena, 'A Diary's Secret', *Country Life,* 12 October 2011, pp 76–9.
Haslam, Richard, 'The Houses of H. Avray Tipping I, *Country Life,* 6 December 1979, pp.2154–7.
Haslam, Richard, 'The Houses of H. Avray Tipping II', *Country Life,* 13 December 1979, pp 2270–3
Singleton, H.G., 'H. Avray Tipping in Monmouthshire', *Severn and Wye Review,* Vol.2 (1970-71), pp 43–7
'Country Cottages and their Gardens. Illustrated by C.E.Mallows' *The International Studio,* Vol.XXXIX. No 156. February 1910
The Editor, 'Bending flower stems are of high decorative value in the garden', *The Garden*, 12 March 1921, pp 130–1.

ACKNOWLEDGEMENTS

Many people have made the writing of this book enjoyable. I would particularly like to thank the owners of Mounton House for encouraging me to write the book and for their generosity in giving time and support throughout the process. Their careful attention to detail over the course of the last twenty years has achieved a spectacular renovation of the house and gardens, redeeming the original hopes of H. Avray Tipping; he would have been immensely grateful to them.

Others were generous in sharing their time and knowledge and by lending photographs, watercolours and archives. I would particularly like to thank Hugh Kitchin, Hugh Holden, Barry Moss, Shaun Earle, Arne Maynard, John Summers, Stephen Horton and also John Campbell, who took all the new photographs. At Lund Humphries my thanks go to Val Rose, Sarah Thorowgood, Alex Batten, Robert Davies, Anna Norman and Adrian Hunt. At home, while I was distracted by the book, Kelly Weare and Rhys Williams kept the High Glanau garden going and ready for garden tours and visitors.

Finally, thanks go to my family: my husband Hilary, and our children Georgina, Willoughby and Henry, who remained patient and enthusiastic through many weeks as the story of Mounton House unfolded.

IMAGE CREDITS

Photography © John Campbell (Room of Light), except for the following:

© Alamy: figs 1, 3, 8, 14, 19, 94
© Arne Maynard Garden Design: figs 169, 171
© CLPL: figs 4, 12, 13, 16, 23, 24, 27, 28, 30–3, 35–7, 39, 43–6, 48, 50, 52, 54, 56, 57, 60–5, 67, 69–74, 76, 79, 81–6, 90, 91, 96, 99–101
© William Collinson: fig.170
© Helena Gerrish: figs 6, 10, 53, 59, 75, 80, 114, 115
© Cyril Hoare: figs 7, 25
© Earle Architects: figs 113, 116–22, 124, 125–8, 133, 135, 136, 138–43, 145–7
© Future Publishing Ltd: figs 17, 22, 26, 58, 88, 111
© Hugh Holden: page 4; figs 104, 105, 107, 108
© Stephen Horton: figs 5, 18, 72, 78, 106
© Hugh Kitchin: figs 20, 21, 29
© Mary Evans Picture Library: figs 15, 77, 87
© MonLife Heritage Museums: figs 68, 110
© Peter Moon: fig.11
© Barry Moss: fig.112
© RHS Lindley Collections: fig.89
© RIBA Collections: figs 34, 47, 102, 103
© Studio Magazine: fig.109
© Wiltshire Museum, Devizes: fig.9

INDEX

NB: Numbers in *italics* indicate images.

Abakanowicz, Magdalena *150*, 151
Adam, Robert 52
Allt y bela (Monmouthshire) 162
Arts and Crafts movement/style 21, 42, 44, 45, *59*, 89, 95, 112, 113, 115, *118*
Aslet, Clive 44
Avray, Henry 95

Bishops of Llandaff 16
Blow, Detmar 42
Brasted Place (Kent) 11, *13*, 14, 16, 41, 42, 52, 72, 89, 151
   urn from 72, 151, 180, *182–3*, 189
Brinsop Court (Hertfordshire) 45, *48*, *49*, 58
British Museum 27
Bryanston (Dorset) 44
Bulbeck Foundry 134, *140–1*
Burdett, Sir Francis 14

Chastleton (Oxfordshire) 57
Chateau de Ville d'Avray 11, *12*
Chelsea Flower Show 161
Chepstow 15, 27, 35, 42, *68*, 95, 111
Chequers (Buckinghamshire) 76, *78–9*, 91
Como cathedral plaque 120, *126–7*
Compton End (Hampshire) 22
Congreve, Lady Celia 11, 76, 91
Conway, Sir Martin 42, 44, 45, 52, 57, 58, 89
Country Life magazine 11, 15, 20, 21, 27, 28, 30, 32, 41, 42, 44, *44*, 45, 67, 68, 73, 75, 89, 91, 134, 162
   first issue 21
   First World War effort 91, *91*
   launch of 21
   Mounton House and gardens articles 42–44, *44*, 57, 67, 68, 73, 75, 90, 104, 134, 162
   offices 21, 27–8, *28*
   Tipping as architectural editor 15, 27, 42, 44, 95
   see also Hudson, Edward (publisher)
Crownwall Developments 111, *113*

Dartington Hall (Devon) 95
Darwin, Bernard 27
Dawber, Sir Guy 42
Deanery Garden, Sonning 20, 21, 29, 75
Decourcy Finance 111
Diana statue *70*, 151, *160*, 161, *190*, *191*
Dictionary of National Biography 12, 14, 15
Dorset Square house (London) 42, 95
Duret, Francisque-Joseph *80*, 81

Earle Architects, commission of 112, 134
   see also Mounton House: restoration
East Cliff (Gloucestershire) 42, *43*
Edwards, Ralph 21, 27, 28
electrical lighting 56–7
Evans, Frederick 28

First World War 11, 91, 95
   assassination of Archduke Franz Ferdinand 89
   conscription 91
Forest of Dean 35
Francis, Eric Carwardine 42, *42*, 45, 56, 57, 91, 95, 112, 115

Garden, The magazine 20, 21, 30, 32, 67, 70, 142, 163
   articles on Mounton House garden 67, 70, *83*, 142, 163
   see also Robinson, William (owner)
Gilpin, William 15
Goldsmith, Oliver 90
Gordon, Home 89
Gordon, Lady Edith 89
Grand Tour 15
Great Western Railway 15
Guanock House (Lincolnshire) 162

Hampton & Sons 104, *106*
Harbrook Cottage (Wiltshire) 14, *14*
Harefield House (Middlesex) 95, *102*
Hennebique, François 56
Henson, A.E. 28, 67, *68*
High Glanau 42, *43*, 44, 95, 96, *96–7*, *98–9*, *100–101*
Holden family 96
Housing Reform Company 35
Hudson, Edward 20, 21, 27, 28, 29, 91
   home at Queen Anne's Gate, London 21, *23*, 28
   see also Country Life magazine
hunting 14

Iford Manor (Wiltshire) 29, *29*
Inner Temple Gateway (London) 56

Jekyll, Gertrude 20, 21, 28, 29, 42, 67, 75, 76
Jourdain, Margaret 28

Kitchin, George Herbert 21, 22, *22*, 30, 32, 35, 41, *45*

landed gentry 12, 14
Latham, Charles 28
Liddell family 96, 104, *105*
Lindisfarne Castle (Northumberland) 21
Lloyd George, David 44, 89, *90*

Lloyd Wright, Frank 67
London Library 27
London season 14
Long Meadow (Somerset) 42, *43*
Lord Lee 76
Louvre, The 81
Lutyens, Edwin 21, *22*, 29, 42

Maquoid, Percy 28
Markenfield Hall (Yorkshire) 45
Mathern Palace 15, 16, *16*, *17*, *18–19*, 20, 27, 29, 30, 35, 44, 91
Maynard, Arne 134, 161, 162, *162*, 163, *164–5*, 165, 170, 171
Messrs Henry Hope & Sons 48
Momentum Consulting Engineers 113
Mounton House (specific information)
   Como cathedral plaque 120, *126–7*
   conversion into separate dwellings 111, *113*
   conversion to a residential school 104, 107, *108–109*, 129, 134
   cost of building 58
   during First World War 11, 91, 95
   during Second World War 96, 104
   electrical lighting 56–7
   first visitors 38, 44, 89
   gardeners' cottages and drive *44*
   gardens 67
      colonnaded garden *80*, 81, *81*
      Country Life article 67, *73*
      pergola 68, *70*, *71*, *72*, *74*, *75*, 75, *75*, 91, 107, 134, 170, *176*
      resurrection of 161–195
      rock garden 81, *82–3*, *85*, 134, 180, *180*, *184–5*, *186–7*, *188–9*
      tea house 76, *76*, *77*, 81, 104, 107, 142
      water garden 30–1, *31*, 32, *34*, 41, 42, 68, 81, *84*
   Grade II* listed status 107, 111
   Jones's Cottage 35, *37*
   leadwork 48, *51*
   plans 48, 69, *75*
   restoration 112–151, *112–151*
   Sigismondo Pandelfo Malatesta plaque 120, *125*
   staff 11, 89, 90, 96
   use of ferro-concrete 56, 113
   West's Cottage 33, *36*
Mounton (village) 30, *30*

Napoleonic Wars 15
Newnes, George 21

Old Palace (Bromley-by-Bow) 56
Oudolf, Piet 161
Oxford University 11–12
   Christ Church college 11, *14*

paper mills 30
Park Hall (Shropshire) 52
Peto, Harold 29, *29*, 42, 75
Prince of Wales (initials) 56, *57*

Quakerism 11, 35, 42

Racing Illustrated 21
Ramsbury Manor (Wiltshire) 28
Richardson, Tim 161
Robinson, William 20, 21, 30, 42, 67, 75
Rondinone, Ugo 151, 170

Severn Estuary 15, *15*, 30, 161, 170, *172–3*
Shirenewton Hall (Monmouthshire) 96, *105*
Sigismondo Pandelfo Malatesta plaque 120, *125*
Skibo Castle (Sutherland) 44
Society for the Protection of Ancient Buildings 16
Society of Antiquaries of London (FSA) 28
St Pierre Pill 30
Stephen, Leslie 12

Thomas, Sir Percy 104
Tintern Abbey *11*
Tipping, Henry Avray 11, *12*, *17*
   architectural editor role at *Country Life* 15, 27, 42, 44, 95
   birth and early life 11
   death 102, 107
   pocket diary for 1908 27, *28*, 41
   garden design 29, 32, 95
   brothers, loss of 12, 14, 41–2
Tipping family coat of arms/crest 48, *51*, 58, *94*
Tipping, William (father) 11, *13*, 14
Tipping, William Fearon (brother) 14, 41, 95–6, *103*
train travel 28
Trellech estate 91
Turner, J.M.W. *15*

Unwin, Raymond 35

Victoria and Albert Museum 56
Victoria Flour Mills 56
Villa Rosemary, Alpes-Maritimes 75

Walker, Maria (mother) 11, *13*, 16
Weaver, Lawrence 28, 42, 48
Weaver's Flour Mill 56
West Monkton (Somerset) 42
Weston Hall (Hertfordshire) 57
Wilde, Oscar 12
Wyndcliffe Court (Monmouthshire) 42, *43*, 91, 95

First published in 2022 by Lund Humphries

Lund Humphries
Huckletree Shoreditch
The Alphabeta Building
18 Finsbury Square
London, EC2A 1AH
UK
www.lundhumphries.com

Mounton House: The Birth and Rebirth of an Edwardian Country Home
© Helena Gerrish, 2022

All rights reserved

978-1-84822-578-7

A Cataloguing-in-Publication record for this book is available from the British Library. All rights reserved. No part of this publication may be reproduced, stored in a retrieval system or transmitted in any form or by any means, electrical, mechanical or otherwise, without first seeking the permission of the copyright owners and publishers. Every effort has been made to seek permission to reproduce the images in this book. Any omissions are entirely unintentional, and details should be addressed to the publishers.

Helena Gerrish has asserted her right under the Copyright, Designs and Patent Act, 1988, to be identified as the Author of this Work.

Front cover: Garden facade 2022.
Back cover: Front facade Mounton House 1912.
Copyedited by Robert Davies
Designed by Adrian Hunt
Set in Domaine Display and Meno Text
Printed in Estonia

200 (pp. 204–5) The Pergola in September
201 (pp. 205–6) Detail of fig.81, the tea house and environing walls